VISITINGBOB

New
Rivers
Press

50th
Anniversary
1968-2018

VISITINGBOB

Poems Inspired by the Life and Work of Bob Dylan

Foreword
Chris Smither

Editors
Thom Tammaro | Alan Davis

Cover and interior design by Phuriwat Chiraphisit
Cover photo by Elliott Landy, "Bob Dylan, in the living room of his Byrdcliffe home, Woodstock, NY, 1968." Copyright © Elliott Landy/Magnum Photos New York. Reprinted by permission.

The publication of *Visiting Bob: Poems Inspired by the Life and Work of Bob Dylan* is made possible by the generous support of Minnesota State University Moorhead, the Dawson Family Endowment, and other contributors to New Rivers Press.

For copyright permission, please contact Frederick T. Courtwright, The Permissions Company, at 570-839-7477 or permdude@eclipse.net.

New Rivers Press is a nonprofit literary press associated with Minnesota State University Moorhead.

Nayt Rundquist, Managing Editor
Kevin Carollo, Editor
Travis Dolence, Director
Thomas Anstadt, Co-Art Director
Trista Conzemius, Co-Art Director

Publishing Interns: Trevor Fellows, Laura Grimm, Kendra Johnson, Anna Landsverk, Mikaila Norman, Lauren Phillips, Ashley Thorpe, Cameron Schulz, Rachael Wing.

The editors of *Visiting Bob* are especially grateful to Kendra Johnson and Rachael Wing, New Rivers Press interns, who worked tirelessly as our assistants from the beginning of the project to its end. Their diligence and timeliness kept us sane and the project on schedule. And Sarah Beck—thank you, too!

 Printed in the USA on acid-free, archival-grade paper.

Visiting Bob: Poems Inspired by the Life and Work of Bob Dylan is distributed nationally by Small Press Distribution.

 New Rivers Press
c/o MSUM
1104 7th Ave S
Moorhead, MN 56563
www.newriverspress.com

"The point isn't to figure him out but to take him in."
—Sam Shephard (note #10 *Poets and Professors*)

"Dylan is about the Individual against the whole of creation"
—Allen Ginsberg, "Is About"

"I can write you poems"
—Bob Dylan, "High Water (For Charley Patton)"

Contents

Foreword Chris Smither

By the time Bob Dylan came to my attention, most of the foundations of my life as a guitar-playing singer had been formed and poured. In 1963, I was an 18 year-old guitar player, raised in New Orleans, addicted to Lightnin' Hopkins and Mississippi John Hurt, mocked by my contemporaries both for playing acoustic guitar and for listening to "old time music," intensely aware that 1500 miles away, up in the Northeast, unreachable, was a hotbed of musical interest and innovation that I desperately wanted to be a part of. And I was almost, but not quite, resigned to the idea that it was just a pipe-dream.

In the end, though, I did get there, not through any sort of remarkable event or manifestation of divine will, but through the kind of stumbling, erratic, one-foot-in-front-of-the-other compulsion that has been the salvation and destruction of countless lives before me and after me. But what was remarkable, still is remarkable, is that there is one voice, a voice that famously refused to be "the voice of a generation," that followed, led, chronicled, foretold, almost every step of the way, in spite of himself. Not because he was telling me in particular, but because I was particularly listening.

Bob Dylan, confronted by media people early in his career, people seeking nothing more than to put an "inspected by" stamp on his forehead, quickly realized that he was facing one more quasi-authoritarian figure demanding, "Explain yourself, young man!" He answered, and has continued to answer over decades, that he *has* explained himself, and that it is not up to him to make you understand the explanation.

"The song *is* the explanation," I would say, years later, "as clear as I can make it, and when you ask me to explain it you are telling me that I failed," knowing as I say it that it will never be as concise or cool as the model, the exemplar. Nor will it be dismissed as enigmatic, which is another way of saying it's cool.

When Bob Dylan was awarded the Nobel Prize I thought, "Hey, someone who does what I do just got the Nobel." But then he did what I *might* have thought to do in a burst of *esprit de l'escalier*. He held back, stayed on the outside looking in until he judged, rightly in my opinion, that he had at least as much presence as did what was on offer, that he could not be co-opted. *The artist is under no obligation to explain himself...*

The poets included in this collection want no explanations from Dylan; they are busy, if anything, using him to explain themselves. These are the people who could hold entire conversations using only Dylan quotes and a few conjunctions. Some of them are people who first realized that the *words* count when they first listened to Dylan. That the way it's said is as important as what is said. They *get* it, and reading them makes me feel that I am in very congenial company. It's all here, the blood on the tracks as well as the tracks in the blood. Behold.

Hal Ackerman **Bob Dylan and Me**

It's a low dank day in November.

Snow or something worse is gathering across the Hudson.

You're crossing a concrete playground in the West Village.

Swing sets and monkey bars stand idle as wallflowers.

The basketball courts are empty except for one person shooting hoops.

He's *supposedly* up at Woodstock recovering from the motorcycle thing,

But clear as shit this is him.

You turn up the fleece-lined collar of your jacket,

Hunch your shoulders and jam your hands into your pockets

Like the album cover.

You change course. You stop at the foul line and wait for a bounce pass.

You want to touch something he's touched.

You want to feel the current, know how he knows things.

You want him to share the stone with you.

He dribbles by without looking and clangs a clumsy hook shot off the rim.

You hate to be the one to say it,

But the "moral conscience of your generation" shoots like a fucking girl.

Aiming,

Squinting,

And he's wearing *motorcycle* boots.

Show some respect for the game, Bob.

He throws up a stumbling one-hander.

The ball thuds hard off the backboard and somehow slams through.

The net is made of bicycle chains

That swish, like the sound of Copa Cabana dance girls

Doing something in unison with beads.

"A little one-on-one?" you suggest.

You get no answer

So you try some abstract humor.

"How about a little two-on-none?"

He takes out a notebook and writes it down, and you say,

"What the hell? I'm here to glom from you!"

And the fucker writes that down too.

You catch a glimpse of his notebook before he shoves it into his pocket.

Everything's written in Japanese.

Top to bottom in rows, like he painted it.

Liz Ahl **Dylan Plugs in at Newport**

Maybe he didn't put it in the best way. Maybe he was rude. But he shook us.
—Jim Rooney

The crackle of the amp, the whine. The thunk
of the pickup sliding home. The unthinkable.
The first pluck sounded like a big *fuck you*
to Pete Seeger, who cowered, hands clapped
to his ears, rocking back and forth in disbelief.

The flat electric guitar body looked soulless,
and the crowd thought they were getting flipped
the bird by that long, skinny neck he fingered
to "Maggie's Farm." And who were these friends
of Dylan, these black men backing him up
with music and bodies that didn't fit?
What did he think he was doing?

It is said the crowd booed him, but the evening
sounded more like a wail, a noise of panic and confusion.
The sound the rabbit makes only when it's dying
in the jaws of the murderous dog.

The decade snapped open like a cracked skull.

What poured out looked like a bad marriage—

the folkie soul and the rock and roll moves.

Joan Baez and Ike Turner. That bad.

Later we would love him more for pushing us over,

for the elbow in the guts, the unrelenting riff

and jangle, but that night we couldn't say

what we saw and heard; that long ago night

when possibility bled once more

from an artist's fingers, slid from his throat.

When, once more, we groaned against it,

we threw up our hands, we resisted.

Robert Alexander **Prose Poem on a Line by Bob Dylan**

As Dylan said, country music stations play soft, distance tuning them out as we drive north, still winter here, snow on the ground. Finally there is silence and static, the last station from somewhere out of state fading entirely. We spend a final few minutes driving along dark roads in the beginning of a spring blizzard.

The hotel seems once to have been a saloon, with rooms above the bar. The owner, a Polish woman in her sixties, has a passion for plants. We exchange a few words in the hall. How do you manage to grow such plants all the way up here? Tropical growths a yard across sprout green in the drafty halls, the small rooms. An asparagus fern is the largest I've ever seen indoors, a rubber plant stretches across two windows, philodendra creep into corners and across ceilings. I tell her it's the love inside her and we smile at each other on our way to the well-furnished bedroom: a rocking chair with floor-standing ashtray, a hand-woven carpet, a huge schefflera, and an uncurtained window looking out on Norway pine and a woodshed. Wagon tracks, white with snow, curve into the dark forest. Somewhere a dog barks, once, twice.

At night I'm with you in an island wilderness, a canyon a sluggish river flows through. Enormous birds are circling overhead.

Joel Allegretti **Epitaph: Edie Sedgwick**

Everyone knew she was the real

heroine of "Blonde on Blonde."

— Patti Smith

I the neon silkscreen the electric love song,

C21H23NO5 on a celluloid spool.

Comet tails draw the letters of my name,

And all, all is silver, for I shine like silver,

Am silver, a million minnows in the shallows

Refracting a sunbeam.

We are here not to be but to do; what I do is shine.

My light, more than the moon's,

Bites into darkness as if it were a tea cake.

Skylines – New York! Paris! – dull before me,

For I shine like silver, am silver,

And so will I shine   forever.

Note: C21H23NO5 is the chemical formula for heroin.

Devon Balwit **Spinning Bob**

In your grandmother's house, the men play Poker and the women
Canasta. She wears a girdle ribbed with whalebone, a padded
brassiere, stockings, a slip. Every day, your grandfather knots
himself into his tie, clacks shut his briefcase, and drives to work
while she stays home and irons his underwear. Your mother picks
you up on weekends in a car painted rainbow. Her mini skirt rides
up over her thighs. She smells of sex and patchouli. While she and
her boyfriend disappear behind shut doors, you leaf through her albums,
reach for Bob, the disc spinning you forward in time to when the meat
of you will have been cracked free of the shell that surrounds you.
Someone will have taken you in his teeth. This will happen in a place
where no two houses look the same, where no one watches *Laugh-In*.
You will interlace fingers, speak to each other in a torrent of rhyme, take
hits off the same joint until the blaze from the race riots cools to ash,
and no one's number is drawn for the draft. The dogs will stop barking
at the marchers, and you will know what it is you are called to do.
Until then, you play your favorite tracks again and again, mouthing
the words that free you from each cage in which you find yourself.

Aliki Barnstone **Bob Dylan, Joan Baez, and a Mystical Child**

1   The first Bob Dylan record I listened to over and over, *Nashville Skyline,* was my parents' in 1969.
     I was a mystical child.

2   Fall of '75: to score tickets to Rolling Thunder Revue, my friend and I camped before dawn on
     a Providence sidewalk, dry leaves blowing from gutters into our hair. The war was over. Later I
     recalled Rolling Thunder carpet-bombed Vietnam.

3   Cobalt glass candlesticks.
     Cobalt Mexican wine glasses brimming
     with purple-microdot-spiked wine.

     We're tangled up in blue sheets—candlelight
     releases flocks of tiny doves skimming
     the wine dark sea rippling and swirling

     moonless
     starry, starry night.

4   *Your eyes are like two jewels in the sky.*
     —sapphire, peridot, amber, tiger eye,
     depending on the lover.

5   I wasn't gonna serve someone or anyone,
    no man, no devil, no lord.

6   Now I carry a rosewood rosary in my purse, purchased in the Ironbound District of Newark from
    a Portuguese woman with eyes like blue topaz.

7   I loved Joan Baez just as much. My lover played jazz guitar naked, then put Billie Holiday on
    the turntable and played my whole length stretched out on a mattress on the floor. I broke it off
    when he almost said my poetry was lousy, not quite. Was it for vanity's sake or to keep a thief
    from breaking me and stealing my art? There would be no diamonds for me, no laying up
    treasures moth and rust corrupt, but I lay up a few days in Providence, a few memories in rust
    belt heaven, where my heart is.

8   Civilization lessons wait in the ark.
    Unroll them to hear God's thunder,
    our faces become blank with light,
    having spoken with the Most High
    face-to-face.

9   Bob Dylan sang in whiteface, his eyes lined with kohl. Joan Baez sang, her spine straight as the
    flowering rod, her short hair a halo in spotlights, her voice rising with the psalmist, where "the
    birds of heaven dwell."

10   Nights I was like Isis, a mystical child and no mystical wife, I woke to the chill beneath the

blankets, Providence wind-tunes droning from the cracks in the windowsills. I shifted away from

him, from loyalty, and could not stay another night.

11   I stood at the soap-scummed sink,

brushed on the midnight eyeliner

he drunkenly swore

made me like a whore.

"Let's go down to the Silvertop Diner," I said.

"One more cup of coffee for the road."

Marge Barrett **Stone Poem**

I bike along the boulders
        by Franconia's basalt cliffs,
            Bob Dylan's song
                ringing in my head,
                    and the poem
                about Nancy Hanks,
            Abe Lincoln's mom,
        who called her son
a rolling stone.
Didn't he
        craggy and gravelly,
            gritty,
                on his own,
                    grind down to granite,
                        smooth,
                    solid,
                revolving,
            resolving,
        releasing us
with a direction home?
Down below,
        a complete unknown,
            I pick pebbles
                from the shore,
                    skip-spin some
                across
            the St. Croix River,
        plunge rudimentary rock
into sedimentary sand.
Ripples swirl
        concentric circles,
            sparkling grains
                of quartz and shale,
                    whirl, twirl—
                how does it feel
            to be on your own—
        then crush,
    crumble,
submerge with
    the swiftly
        flowing stream,
            like a rolling stone.

Anne Becker **Lament for Bob Dylan**

...as if he were holding the sea in
his black hands,
as if, after giving him all that power,
she now could give him pity and
consolation...

—Gerald Stern, "The Same Moon Above Us"

Lament, lament for Hibbing, for Duluth,
    lament for Marquette, for Munising, for the Sault;
Let me lament the raw earth, its skin scraped off;
Lament for the grass pulled up by the roots;
Lament, lament for the pure child, the pure dirt;
Let me lament the sheer rain of words—each pure
    note harnessed to the right word;
Let me lament, let me lament, let me lament for the electrician's
    son with the sizzling hair, song searing the mouth, cracking
    the lips, lament caught in the throat;
Let me lament the swirl of ash on the tongue, the charred word;
Let me lament the eagle's beak rotted with poison, lament blowing
    through the nose, wind in a ruin;
Blistered tear, smooth cheek—let me lament the downy hair
    on the young neck, the suspicious eyes, the walking debt;
Let me lament the dumb repetition of hunger.
    faithful generations of want;
Lament, lament for the gate open and shut;
Lament, lament for the locked box of luck;

Lament for the rain both inside and out;
Lament for the money borrowed and stunned;
For the rank cruelty and unintended harm;
For the useless car and the wailing fire truck—
         for the *phony false alarm*—
Lament for the stiff mask strayed from the shelf;
         and for the electric son plugged in, playing himself;
For the risky kitchen where you freeze, where you bake—
         weep for real pain—the phantom ache—
Lament for the authorities, for the agents, for the brakeman,
         for the promoters, lament for the undertaker, the agitators,
         the commissioners, the free-loaders, lament for the sword
         swallower, the throat-borrower, for the war horse, the riot
         squad, lament for the scentless roses;
Lament for the pillar of salt corroding in the sun, he thought he had
         everything, he never looked back—he didn't know what he'd done;
And for wise incorruptible love—gone like ice—gone like air—
         lament for the quivering bridge;
Lament, lament for the angel visions of Johanna—were they hers?
         Were they his? Were they mine? Were they yours?
Lament for the harm done unto you, the harm you did;
Lament for the love done wrong, time mislaid, scratched
         face at the window, rain tracks on the pane;
Wolf moans at the blue door—jowl sagging, smoldering eye—his one
         song—his sole idea of order;
And woe sing the wholly free, released from the strings of the body; Let me lament the
busted windows of the sea;

And for the ship stalled at the shore, deranged harpoon,
 impostor cabin boy, manic crew;
Lament for the engine, lament for the sail, for the bowline,
 for the mast, lament for the whale;
And the delusional captain adrift in the dunes—
 his fevered pockets—his drunken shoe—
Fire thirsts, unquenchable, guzzling the parched air,
 tomorrow's long past, the hours rust—
And the little boy lost in the blinding snow, bitter cold, smoking eyelids,
 fire, the fire full of holes;
Lament for the north country, jumping off place, end of the
 world, mine's closed, the borderline's blurred;
For the bootless weatherman, the aimless wind—
 and for the *ghost of electricity* whistling its scorched hymn;
Lament, lament for the ground, insects that play there, delicate
 snake in the weeds, the purposeful ants, lizards,
 turtles, everything that breathes;
Lament for the National Guard guarding the wrong door, for the bored slave,
 the *homesick sailors,* half-lit ladies, escape artist,
 crumbled fortress, cold Joker, traitor kiss;
Let me lament the strangled voice cut off of the vine,
 lament for the words that have shriveled and died;
Lament for the homeless, the ruthless, the witless, the clueless,
 the deathless, the reckless, the eyeless, the foolish;
Let me lament the pale night, the black daytime,
 lament for the feckless nickel, the friendless dime;
Let me note the little red hen's lament, and the evil step-sisters' lament, and

the great ape and the little elves dancing their lament;
Lament, lament for this old man, his house full of knick-knacks, his single
thumb, his dog Bingo, his nameless furious wife;
Lament, lament for the mutilated mice, the triumphant cheese, lone-
some cornbread, juicy frog, the innocent knife;
Let me lament, let me lament, let me lament for the hoodlum persuaders
of song—scattered dust—desolate carnival boys, their wild
high-wire rhymes, their sisters' speechless science;
Lament, lament for the low ringing of the law;
Lament for the tambourine giant, the silver saxophones and the flutes;
Lament for Jack-a-Diamonds, for Gypsy Davy, for Mr. Jones "Don't-Know-What's-Happening-Do-You,"
for the cocky punks, the plucky
scoundrels, the scorned lovers, the *jealous monk;*
Lament for the city of truth spoken in song;
Pity the shadow of the laughter of youth—burned—gone—

their god knocked
down—the ikon broken—rattle bag of bones and polka dot rag—already
the prophets mourn—the robin falls mute—and the dove—and the raven—
black fire flailing her unfeathered wings—their illegible scrawl—soft white
underbelly of the brain—tick of the heart hung in its sac,
roiling, swollen—golden drop of sweat;
And the windowsill and the tattered ceiling—
And the cowboy angel astride his cloud-horse, twirling his lariat candle;
And the renegade physicist fiddler, fiddling in anger;
Naked emperor at the edge, howling for his lost dominion, his soldier-clowns stuck in
the coffin phone booth;
And his junkyard bed, its skeleton mattress, his black tooth;

And *Maggie's farm,* what she grew there, her lunatic ma, her raging
        pa, her cerebral servant, her well-scrubbed floor;
And Rita and Annie, and Mona and Louise, all the saints in the penitentiary;
Let me lament for the 18, for the 30, the 50 years' wait;
Lament for the price you paid—what you had to say—what you were offered,
        what you didn't get straight;
Let me note every lament and lament each note:

                                        Let me lament
                the choked wind, the dry rain
                the shattered hand and the wall
                a shell,   a shard,   salt   sand
                unmanned man   the endless highway's end
                lion's breath   footsteps silent   abandoned name . . .

                                letmelament letmelament letmelament
                                letmelament letmelament, letmelament

Ah mama, can this really. . .

                                the golden bead of sweat

letmelament, letmelament letmelament

Madeleine Beckman **Bob in Brown Corduroys**

It wasn't a cliché summer night

when we met at a sweaty bar

with no a/c

you drinking a beer

me—bad white wine.

We were waiting for Muddy Waters

still backstage.

How could *you* not get onstage?

And you did. Excused yourself from the bar

and our conversation about Muddy   and

impromptu   with Scarlett, her violin

the others

you practically blew the doors off that place.

After jamming on stage,

we all headed for Victoria Spivey's place

no clue how we got there but we did.

Smoked & drank, laughed & danced.

I was happy—and having fun.

It was a night full of rhythm and good feelings.

I went to the bedroom—for lipstick or something

in my handbag on the bed

and turned to see you standing just inside the door

You're a good dancer, you said.

Hmm... ok.

Then you asked for my number

and I figured, sure, and scratched it down

on the inside of a matchbook cover.

We visited each other

me to your place on McDougal Street

you to my loft on Chambers Street

above a Chicken Delight fast food shop.

Not quite sure how you shimmied up so fast

that trapeze hanging from the ceiling in my loft

like you belonged there—but you did.

You traveled a lot that summer and fall

preparing for that tour you invited me on

but I declined.

(Sometimes we make dumb decisions.)

Where are you calling from, I'd ask.

Laredo, or *Durango*.

Wait til you hear this song I'm writing.

You were right – made me smile

as you played and sang into the phone.

When you'd call the smoking clinic

("Stop Smoking Now!") where I worked,

the receptionist, thinking she was funny, would say:

Lay lady lay...you got a call while you were in session.

One night when we were talking

over Afghan chicken

I cooked that wasn't spicy enough for you

but destroyed my tongue   you said:

You've got to go up to Harlem

visit Mrs. Jamison. She's a voodoo psychic.

Very powerful...she sees things.

So, I went to Harlem. Stood on the stoop of a brownstone

every window – top to bottom boarded up.

I knocked a few times. No answer.

When I saw two men looking down at me

from an upstairs window of a bombed out building—

I bolted.

No Mrs. Jamison to tell *my* future.

You and I liked drawing together with pencils.

Anything would do: wine bottles, plates,

that trapeze, left over chicken bones.

What is that? You asked incredulously.

The wine bottle and plates, I replied.

They don't look like that. Draw what you see.

So I started again.

Marvin Bell **The Book of the Dead Man**

(Dylan's Names)

Live as if you were already dead.

> —Zen admonition

All I can do is be me, whoever that is.

> —Bob Dylan

1. About the Dead Man and Dylan's Names

Who were Elston Gunn and Blind Boy Grunt, Bob Landy and Robert Milkwood Thomas, Tedham
      Porterhouse and Lucky Wilbury, Boo Wilbury and Jack Frost, who was Sergei Petrov?

When the Swedish Academy gave him the Nobel, the grumps got huffy and, wouldn't you know it,
      the squares got hip.

Ah, but the dead man is the one who knows what it's worth and what it's not worth, so too the
      performer who thought up "The Never Ending Tour."

The dead man knows that being a grownup means knowing that things end.

The dead man understands in his bones that a lifetime is an interlude, not yet a flagged sixteenth in
      a century of whole notes.

To bend the genres as Dylan did meant holding up the sky and spending his reserves.

We do not ask for propriety when the music starts, nor for civic good, nor do we await the return of
      sounds traveling a spherical universe.

We do not ask the music of the spheres to notate the progression of dissonance to harmony and
      back, it would take forever.

Who is Bob Dylan, and who was Bob Dylan, and who will have been Bob Dylan?

It is not incumbent upon the artist to know, nor need a witness come forth.

2. *More About the Dead Man and Dylan's Names*

The Dead Man holds that what are known as the blues are only the first blues, and that hands-up gospel, the lost souls of country, the rebellious arousal of rock, and the helpless loves of The Great American Songbook are also the blues.

The Dead Man will not argue in words, for music always wins.

It's the Dylan of true rhymes, iambics, songs that go on breathing where others stopped, choruses that became marching orders—not the staging, but a voice like straw and lungs like an accordion that could not stop.

The Dead Man, like Dylan, does not linger in expectation, he too changes keys and forms, he lightly sings his lines and hums in private, waiting for the new thing to find him.

No one knows better than the Dead Man the backward looks of an audience that craves the all-time favorites.

The Dead Man is neither a fanboy nor a follower, but is out front with his ears open.

He knows it when he hears and sees it—music breaking through the noise, and the analysts in wet shoes.

When lightning hits, the critics simmer and fizzle.

The Dead Man knows that for the artist who reimagines himself some luck is bad luck, as are some places, so why stay there?

Not to remain a Zimmerman, then, who may be the backstage usher who tells his children he once met you.

Tara Betts **When Dylan Woke to George Jackson's Death**

Sometimes I think this whole world
is one big prison yard.
Some of us are prisoners.
The rest of us are guards.

—Bob Dylan

That August 1971 morning, Dylan could have been rattled
alive and shaken with everything the Panthers could have
told him, and Angela Davis bold soft-spoken tenets raking
across his grief when he lifted his pen and pressed letters
into words on paper. Some blues fell out of his grief to say
Lord, Lord because the prison guards shot Jackson to death
bleeding and without a single weapon. The ballad closed
on every verse that a life sentence is not equal to $70 stolen,
much less his life, that George never lived on his knees, so
Dylan echoed what the black folks knew, he would not bow.

Robert Bly **Driving West in 1970**

My dear children, do you remember the morning

When we climbed into the old Plymouth

And drove west straight toward the Pacific?

We were all the people there were.

We followed Dylan's songs all the way west.

It was Seventy; the war was over, almost;

And we were driving to the sea.

We had closed the farm, tucked in

The flap, and were eating the honey

Of distance and the word "there."

Oh whee, we're gonna fly

Down into the easy chair. We sang that

Over and over. That's what the early

Seventies were like. We weren't afraid.

And a hole had opened in the world.

We laughed at Las Vegas.

There was enough gaiety

For all of us, and ahead of us was

The ocean. Tomorrow's

The day my bride's gonna come.

And the war was over, almost.

John Bradley **Bob Dylan at the Typewriter**

Who's this skinny kid. Bob. Hammering away. On the typewriter. Cig in hand.

Typing: *This machine fights fascism. But not so good. As Lead Belly's guitar.*

Or. *Woody Guthrie. Was born. With twelve fingers. And a long. Prehensile tail.*

Or. *Oh Betty. Black Betty. Where can I find. In Dinkytown. Your bam-da-lam.*

Or. *What say. Hank Williams. We ride the rails. Fore winter. Comes messin round.*

Not one quarter do you last. Not nearly enough. Universe. In the university.

The Ten O'Clock Scholar. Field Holler High. That was school. For a young rounder.

Oh Betty. Black Betty. Let's hop a freight. Bound for Woody. Bam-da-lam.

Typing. By day. The new name. *Robert Presley. Bob Holly. Bobby Lee Lewis.*

And then. *Bob Dillon.* Not the poet. But Sheriff Matt Dillon's. Bastard son.

Born of tumbleweed boxcar snake oil whisky dance hall juke joint levee revival tent.

Now. You're called *Barry Manilow.* By some skinny punk. At the *Minnesota Daily.*

Michael Brockley **Aloha Shirt Man Takes a Facebook Quiz to Match Him with a Woman from a Bob Dylan Song, and Wins a Date with Rosemary**

He arrives at her condo in a DeLorean borrowed from Marty McFly, wearing a black Hawaiian shirt pinkened with flamingos. She still looks like a queen without a crown. The couple swings by a scene in *Pat Garrett and Billy the Kid to* scramble the cans of beans Alias spent an afternoon arranging. Afterward they dine on fugu sashimi in Ruthie's honky-tonk lagoon. Their thoughts are dirty. They're tangled up in blue. Aloha Shirt Man wants a lover like a raven with a broken wing; Rosemary just needs to kill a judge. The time machine accelerates through a stop sign on Lincoln County Road, beyond the gravity of crying trains, beyond the blandishments of the goddess of gloom. Aloha Shirt Man passes gallows and train wrecks. Ignores the Jack of Hearts hitchhiking through an idiot wind. Beside him, Rosemary juggles her knives, admiring her reflection in the spinning mirrors of the blades. She reroutes the DeLorean to the judge on Highway 5. Wants to hang something on her wall. But the drifters stay too long in Mississippi plotting floods and fires. Until Rosemary throws her panties out the window eloping with a jingle-jangle man with a platinum satchel. Leaving Aloha Shirt Man gripping the steering wheel of a Buick 6, trapped between his blues and his desires.

Nicole Brooks **Because Bob Dylan**

Because Bob Dylan is my boyfriend

I never tire of his ranting about conquerors

those who write the strong sentences

whose knuckles never scrape the ground.

Bob's a full bright glass-blown jester in his jeans

and curly Q hair, sipping 3 AM grit coffee between outbursts

in a diner around the corner from our Village sanctum.

Bob can't be heard in the bars, so most nights we stay home

and drink beer and I clean his guitars

while he writes songs in a faded red spiral-bound.

Flecks of white paper float down to the Persian rugs like fat doves.

He yells out to me, "Baby, count me a waltz. Count me a 1, 2, 3, a 1, 2, 3."

On Sundays Bob and I lie in bed a whole day. We talk of conspiracies,

mysteries, the Martian canals crisscrossing Mars, cryonics societies,

things that fall from the sky fast, furious.

When I go home to Indiana for a visit I call Bob

every day. I leave messages, I wait on the other line

because Bob's talking peace with the government.

Charles Bukowski **trench warfare**

sick with the flu

drinking beer

my radio on loud

enough to overcome

the sounds of the

stereo people who

have just moved

into the court

across the way.

asleep or awake

they play their set at top volume

leaving their

doors and windows

open.

they are each

18, married, wear

red shoes,

are blonde,

slim.

they play

everything: jazz,

classical, rock,

country, modern

as long as it is

loud.

this is the problem

of being poor:

we must share each

other's sounds.

last week it was

my turn:

there were two women

in here

fighting each other

and then they

ran up the walk

screaming.

the police came.

now it's their

turn.

now I am walking

up and down in

my dirty shorts,

two rubber earplugs

stuck deep into

my ears.

I even consider

murder.

such rude little

rabbits!

walking little pieces

of snot!

but in our land

and in our way

there has never

been a chance;

it's only when

things are not
going too badly
for a while
that we forget.

someday they'll
each be dead
someday they'll
each have a
separate coffin
and it will be
quiet.

but right now
it's Bob Dylan
Bob Dylan Bob
Dylan all the
way.

Sidney Burris **An Afternoon with Bob Dylan**

"Yes, I respect his music,
 but I cannot say I like it,"
 you said from our inadequate kitchen
 as I sat in our inadequate den
 and watched an anchorman wander
 towards the notion
 that as long as we know nothing
 nothing is enough.

 Wasn't I listening?
 You'd say it again,
 this time a bit stronger:
 "Yes, of course, I hate his music,
 and what's more, I always hated him."
 I laid my arms on the armchair
 beside the remote control
 and set the anchorman adrift

 in a collapsing point of blue light.
 That's all there was to it,
 a kind of alchemial maxim:
 the screen winked and blackened.
 And no more Dylan on the phonograph.
 We're doing very well with what we've got,
 a way of reducing anyone
 to a quiet little dot.

Edward Byrne **Listening to Dylan with My Son**

Alone you stand with nobody near
When a trembling distant voice, unclear
Startles your sleeping ears to hear
That somebody thinks they really found you...

—Bob Dylan, "It's Alright Ma (I'm Only Bleeding)"

When this evening's northern wind whispers

once more through eaves outside our window,

and much higher bare branches begin to brush

the vinyl siding with winter's irregular rhythm,

we listen again, as if in ritual, to Dylan singing

about times of deep loss and a need to endure.

Due to autism and an inability to place faces

in his mind, isolated for years my son has learned

instead to identify any individual by the defined

sound of a distinct voice that might remind him

of other sources—perhaps a word spoken softly

recalls a birdcall or the rich pitch of a baritone

evokes the almost noble lower notes in some

old automobile horn. Alex always recognizes

Dylan's vocals, even the aging raspy lilt pleases

enough to create a smile, as if each bittersweet

yet lyrical line delivered is filled with a secret

assurance, a shared sense his own scratchy speech,

marked sometimes by a coarse lack of clarity

and language lost in hoarseness, will still reach

those in whom he seeks to confide and will be

received like a lone wolf's cry in the cold night.

David Cappella **Bob Dylan's Vocal Chords**

for Susan O.

The speech pathologist sits on the icy aluminum bench

beside me, as we watch the hockey game, chilly

in the refrigerator cold of the skating rink.

Outside squats a New England heat wave,

one of those cursed Bermuda highs that plants its ass

right on the elbow of the Cape with a heat

that gathers up and stings every toe

of the foot that first sinks into scalding beach sand.

It's a heavy heat that crams the air

back into the throat. And when I clear mine,

just as the crack of her husband's slap shot,

low and mean, snaps an echo to the ceiling,

I say, "I'm going to hear Dylan this weekend."

The speech pathologist shakes her head from side to side.

"How can you listen to him?" she asks me.

I think, *oh no, another 'Dylan's voice' discussion*.

She tells me, "His voice needs some serious rest."

And who can argue with that? The Minstrel is tireless

and I imagine the road must be a blanket party

on his throat. She says, "The problem is the vocal cord lining."

The flying puck whizzes past, thuds against the far corner,

and drops lifeless as I picture The Minstrel after a gig

plopping down exhausted on his tour bus

contemplative, taking a scratchy swallow.

The speech pathologist informs me, without a doubt,

Dylan's vocal cord linings are severely jagged and rough

like barbed wire, that scar tissue and nodules layer

his cords, a result from years of smoking, of drugs,

of attempts at trying to change the sound of his voice.

Dylan, the lion tamer with a whip and a chair, yelling

at his voice, commanding it to jump up and sit on its back legs.

She adds, "A laryngoscopy would show the simple truth."

I learn that the vocal linings are smooth, moist, and supple.

I think of a quahog, but the speech pathologist notes

that if viewed from the mouth down, the linings

look like a vagina. Their folds close into a smooth seal,

but Dylan's cords are so roughly coated

with layer upon layer of crud from years of abuse

and his throat muscles are so tensed up, as though

his larynx is continually being scratched by cat claws,

that Dylan has an imperfect seal and a weak vocal quality.

Perhaps this accounts for the infusion of ecstasy coursing

through my body every time I hear him sing "Desolation Row."

The speech pathologist describes how, at Dylan's concerts,

she used to sit with her fingers in her ears. She tells me

that this bothered her because she still cherishes every word,

every phrase written by The Minstrel. They sing to her

now, as she stares out at the skaters, her rhapsodic gaze,

beatific and stark under the glare of the rink lights.

It is one of those blessed instants, an odd moment

that Dylan himself might note in scribbled lines and then,

during a late set, in some out of way venue

in the middle of the week, conjure those exact words in his throat

and with a long exhale cry them out, tremulous and whiny,

in a sweet new baby wail into the stale, blue air.

Damian A. Carpenter **Bob Dylan Plays
the Cassopolis Pole Barn**

I.

Silage, fermented fodder for ruminants,

Cows that herd like pied, steaming snowdrifts,

Shelter where there is no shelter,

Shelter from the dead-cold chill wind,

Storms across flat, white Michiana fields.

Train, Grand Trunk Western line rollin,

Near on a century, blowin through,

Snowdrifts so high last winter,

Cows walked over the barbed wire,

Like bowling pins, her father said.

Pie safe, protection from hobo fingers,

There since before the tracks were laid,

Train stop at the mill past Prairie Grove,

Rest stop for hungry boxcar savants

On the way to Chicago and its big shoulders.

Could see them cross the half-mile

From the kitchen window, grandmother said.

Summer, throwing stones in Christiana Creek,

A shaded break from mending fences,

Basement Tape noise rising like sun-dazzled mist,

A million dollar bash mending fences,

Throwing stones with too much of nothing

But time to sit and watch the creek flow

As one might punch oneself in the face with his fist

Or swirl a cup of meat while contemplating the sign on the cross.

II.

Years later she'd dream of Dylan playing in the pole barn—

The white one down by the rusted silage conveyor

Where her father hand-milked the cow

Who lost her calf two springs ago—

The 1975 Bob, the one with the white face paint:

A white mask to match the white barn,

A spray of hay rather than flowers in his hat.

No one but her in the audience.

I didn't ask why I wasn't there

Because I had my own dreams.

Like when he played the Andes Hotel in the Catskills

And it wasn't so much the intimate Dylan concert

As the one-on-one conversations

That weren't really conversations

But a tongue-tied silence on my end

And a piercing blue but sympathetic gaze on the other.

Sometimes Bob makes a comment

About cherry pie and mastiffs

And I nod my head and utter a few words.

It didn't matter that I wasn't in her dream nor she in mine

Because we were there in the telling.

She let me be in her dream

And I let her be in mine

The moment on that first meet

While I poured over Guthrie manuscripts

And the siren wail of "Highway 61" from my phone

Shredded the archival silence

And she smiled.

Johnny Cash **Of Bob Dylan**

There are those who do not
   imitate,
Who cannot imitate
But then there are those
   who emulate
At times, to expand further
   the light
Of an original glow.
   Knowing that to imitate
      the living
   is mockery
   And to imitate the dead
   Is robbery
There are those
Who are beings complete unto
   themselves
Whole, undaunted,—a source
   As leaves of grass, as stars

As mountains, alike, alike,
   alike,
Yet unalike
Each is complete and
   contained
And as each unalike star
   shines
Each ray of light is forever
   gone
To leave way for a new ray
And a new ray, as from a
   fountain
Complete unto itself, full,
   flowing.
   So are some souls like stars
   And their words, works and
      songs
Like strong, quick flashes of
   light

From a brilliant, erupting
    cone.
    So where are your
      mountains
      To match some men?
This man can rhyme the tick
    of time
The edge of pain, the what
    of sane
And comprehend the good in
    men, the bad in men
    Can feel the hate of fight,
      the love of right
    And the creep of blight
      at the speed of light
The pain of dawn, the gone
    of gone
The end of friend, the end of end

By math of trend
    What grip to hold what he
      is told
    How long to hold, how
      strong to hold
    How much to hold of what
      is told.
And Know
    The yield of rend; the break
      of bend
    The scar of mend
    I'm proud to say that I
      know it,
    Here-in is a hell of a poet.
    And lots of other things
    And lots of other things.

Jan Chronister **At the Armory in Duluth**

The figure on stage in

suit, tie and white shirt

takes his music seriously

croons a love song to Peggy Sue

Three days later an after-concert flight to Fargo

crashes killing all on board.

They call it the day the music died

but a seventeen-year-old from Hibbing

made sure that didn't happen.

Rocco de Giacomo **To Bob Dylan**

I didn't like you, Bob,

until now.

It wasn't that

you always reminded me of Gonzo

with a head cold

or that

I always imagined your lyrics

scribbled out in purple crayon,

or that

your duet with Janis

sounded more like two cats

making it

under a wicker chair

than two drunks stumbling

through the lyrics of last call.

It's your fans, Bob:

The MasterCard malcontents

sucking back Evian water

between sets at the Superfitness,

digging out their wedgies

as they sweat

and swoon to burned memories

of free love

in the hot mud

of Woodstock.

The driver's side airbags

crooning with their golf buddies,

shaking their nine-irons

at the complacency of kids today

and how

by god

by god

when they were young

they went out

and they made a difference.

And the great,

hippie

den

mothers,

their teenage granddaughters

orbiting them like sour moons,

Chapters-bought, special edition books of your lyrics

crushed to their breasts,

all,

just waiting

—chins wobbling—

waiting for you

to die

so that they can weep

all over you,

and like an episode

of *While You Were Out*

decorate your headstone

with Body Shop Bath candles,

patchouli incense sticks,

and empty 2 litre bottles

of Maria Christina.

However,

in that Victoria's Secret commercial,

I realized, Bob,

that you've been waiting too.

Cast in a cadaver light,

you're a lingering target

for that stray bullet,

that loaded syringe,

or one last hit of whiskey,

that turned Janis, Jimi, and Jim

—those glorious letdowns—

into legends

before what they produced

became products placed

in an unremarkable world:

an empty highway

an open stage

a distant uncle's birthday party:

you were all caught

in riptide of the right moment,

but only you, Bob,

were blessed with the cruel knack

of survival

and in surviving

you fail,

like the rest of us,

and you have to wait, now,

like the rest of us

for that long, slow death,

that awaits everyone.

Theodore Deppe **Coming Home to
the North Country**

First the night train, then the long drive

to Superior for an overdue visit to the past.

In an hour, the temperature fell fifty degrees,

so no surprise that my first home,

reappearing after six decades,

did so beneath hail, beneath lightning.

Then further back, crossing

the bridge to Duluth—

June, but balls of ice on the roadside

like welcoming confetti.

We found the hospital, took the elevator

to the birthing center above the stormy

and shimmering lake. Impossible to go

further back in this world. From the ground

of things, a sudden bright tremor.

*

I knew that Bobby Zimmerman and I

first drew breath in the same hospital,

but I hadn't realized until now

that I was born on Desolation Row.

Once, I might have said that

with a sort of pride,

or played it for the joke,

but I just learned that a few blocks

and thirty years from my birth

our townspeople lynched

three black circus workers.

And yes, they sold postcards

of the hanging, violent images

you can find online, though you may not

want to. I can't stop seeing

the mutilated men. And the faces

in the crowd. Everyone mugging

for the camera. Everyone smiling

on cue for the hangman.

*

We drove north on old Highway 61 to spend

the night in a lighthouse. Deer in the garden,

otter by the shore, and my wife invited me

to a sunset walk on the breakwater.

Halfway, fog barreled in, lightning

in the distance, and the couple in front

turned back. First, a gleaming wedge

of reddish gray erased the jetty's end. Then

we were in it, too, out of sight of land, claimed

by the marvelous. Deep horn

of an ore freighter, faraway thunder, waves

breaking beneath us, and the narrow, wet jetty

made me question going on, but my wife

quoted Dickinson: *If your Nerve, deny you—*

Go above your Nerve.

No way to watch her disappear

alone, so, reciting my given lines,

I followed. Then we stepped through

the cloud curtain—we were out at the end,

everything red-gold and impossibly clear,

and the storm

already a fold in the past's long veil.

*

Arriving too late for anyone to greet us,

we found instructions

signed by *The Lighthouse Ghost*.

One note invited us

to a slice of rhubarb pie. The next warned us

not to play the gramophone. My wife

wound the crank, placed the needle

onto an old 78, and was rewarded

by "West End Blues." The lighthouse,

the music, the furnishings,

all stepped from another era. Was the ghost

watching us disobey? Or did she forget us

after the piano solo, as I forgot almost everything

and concentrated on Louis Armstrong's

one held trumpet note

that hovered in the air with no plans

of ever coming down. It took me six decades

to revisit Highway 61, the long Blues road

that stretches from New Orleans

to the North Country. A sustained note

that follows the Mississippi most of the way,

past the spot where Bessie Smith died,

past the crossroads where Robert Johnson

bargained with the devil, past the square in Duluth

of the three slain circus workers.

As if a man could put everything

he'd loved or lost into one glistening note,

make it cut through time

like a bridge we might walk back and forth on—

a way perhaps to go back even further—

and then gently, safely,

bring all that heartbreak and joy

back down to earth. When the stylus

reached the end of the record's

spiral universe, it orbited the last groove

like a glittering probe turned into space debris.

Lifting it, I moved the little diamond

back to the beginning. Crossed

the forbidden bridge one more time.

Diane di Prima **Revolutionary Letter #4**

Left to themselves people

grow their hair.

Left to themselves they

take off their shoes.

Left to themselves they make love

sleep easily

share blankets, dope & children

they are not lazy or afraid

they plant seeds, they smile, they

speak to one another. The word

coming into its own: touch of love;

on the brain, the ear.

//

We return with the sea, the tides

we return as often as leaves, as numerous

as grass, gentle, insistent, we remember

the way,

our babes toddle barefoot thru the cities of the universe.

Theo Dorgan **The Bodhisattvas That We Were
Are Still On The Road**

Morning, sun in the trees, the road outside Killarney,

first harmonica and learning "Love Minus Zero";

so earnest and clear, the long road before me,

ready for love and learning, ready to go.

Three bows to that very young man.

Three bows to the unquiet spirit of Jack Kerouac,

to the lonely man in the dark nights where he sighs for the road,

wishes the road back again, would like to start over,

a great natural bedfellow lonesome in Carnac at the end

for morning, sun in the trees, the road outside himself,

the words tumbling in his head, love and zero balanced

clear, facing the highway and himself, hearing the long train

pull away into the far-off halls of night.

Three bows to that very young man.

Nel mezzo del cammin, or a little further on,

I stop what I'm doing to let the city roar past me,

to let myself fall all the way back to that morning

where the road began, and farther back—

Cork City Library, checking out *On The Road*,

staying up for a week of nights with the house asleep,

puzzling it all out, the wild hammering swoop of it,

the dizzy rising and falling and unfolding.

So many roads behind me now and the halls of night

getting closer, the starry halls of night; I reach the book

down from the shelves, knock a harmonica to the floor.

I pick it up and blow: "Love Minus Zero/No Limit."

Stephen Dunn **Phantom**

It's the last hour of a final day

in June, my wife sleeping,

Bob Dylan going ninety miles an hour

down a dead-end street,

and moments ago—bless the mind

that works against itself—

Hegel conceding that philosophy

always arrives too late.

Through his cat door

here comes our orange cat,

empty-mouthed, looking bereft.

Voles and mice, don't dare relax.

Loners and dreamers, time to test

the dark, visit the haunts.

I'm waiting for that click

of the tape deck or the chapter's end,

and whichever comes first—one of those

deals you make with yourself.

It's the click. Now I'll take to bed

this body and the phantom

of what it once was, inseparable

as they are these days, smoke

rising from a stubborn fire.

Night light, be my guide.

I can feel my way just so far.

Susan Elbe *Highway 61 Revisited*

When the house lights cut, Dylan, pushing 60

and weird as ever, walks onto a stripped stage,

his skin, through binoculars, anemic

as the light in all-night diners,

his shiny suit, rubbery and tough as roof tar.

He plays lead guitar and starts with

something old, making us feel wistful

for bell-bottom jeans, beaded belts,

hand-tooled sandals, feather earrings,

hashish, and all-night dialogues,

his band and half the audience not yet born

when we believed we'd be forever young.

Stranded here in middle-age, we want to know—

under whose bed did we leave our silk

bikini underpants, at the bottom of what drawer

did we stash a sandwich bag of joints?

Where did we hide all those years?

They still shine inside us

like the rain Louise held in her hands

and this *all seems so cruel*. The future's wick,

a flint struck in the unlit cave of a concert hall,

blue flames held against the gaping dark.

Lawrence Ferlinghetti **The Jack of Hearts**

(for Dylan)

Who are we now, who are we ever,

Skin books parchment bodies libraries of the living

gilt almanacs of the very rich

encyclopedias of little people

packs of player face down

on faded maps of America

with no Jack of Hearts

in the time of the ostrich

Fields full of rooks

dumb pawns in black and white kingdoms

And revolutions the festivals of the oppressed

and festivals the little revolutions

of the bourgeoisie

where gypsy fortune tellers deal

without the Jack of Hearts

the black-eyed one who sees all ways

the one with the eye of a horse

the one with the light in his eye

the one with his eye on the star named Nova

the one for the ones with no one to lead them

the one whose day has just begun

the one with the star in his cap

the cat with future feet

looking like a Jack of Hearts

mystic Jack Zen Jack with crazy koans

Vegas Jack who rolls the bones

the high roller behind the dealer

the one who'll shake them

the one who'll shake the ones unshaken

the fearless one

the one without bullshit

the stud with the straightest answer

the one with blazing words for guns

the distance runner with the word to pass

the night rider with the urgent message

The man from La Mancha riding bareback

The one who bears the great tradition

and breaks it

The Mysterious Stranger who comes & goes

The Jack of Hearts who speaks out

in the time of the ostrich

the one who sees the ostrich

the one who sees what the ostrich sees in the sand

the one who digs the mystery

and stands in the corner smiling

like a Jack of Hearts

at the ones with no one to lead them

the ones with their eyes in the sands

the sand that runs through the glass

the ones who don't want to look

at what's going down around them

the shut-eye ones who wish

that someone else would seize the day

that someone else would tell them

which way up and which way out

and whom to hate and whom to love

like Big Jack groovy Jack the Jack of light

Sainted Jack who had the Revelations

and spoke the poem of apocalypse

Poet Jack with the light pack

who travels by himself

and leaves the ladies smiling

Dharma Jack with the beatitudes

drunk on a bus addressing everyone

the silent ones with the frozen faces

the ones with *The Wall Street Journal*

who never speak to strangers

the ones that got lost in the shuffle

and never drew the Jack of Hearts

the one who'd turn them on

who'd save them from themselves

the one who heals the Hamlet in them

the silent Ham who never acts

the dude on the corner in two-tone shoes

who knows the name of the game

and names his game

the kid who paints the fence

the boy who digs the treasure up

the boy with the beans on the beanstalk

the dandy man the candy man

the one with the lollipops

the harlequin man

who tells the tic-toc man to stuff it

in front of the house that Jack built

where sleeps the Cock that crowed in the morn

where sleeps the Cow with the crumpled horn

where sleeps the dude who kept the horse

with the beautiful form

and kissed the Maiden all forlorn

the Jack of the pack all tattered and torn

the one the queen keeps her eye on

Dark Rider on a white horse

after the Apocalypse

Prophet stoned on the wheel of fortune

Sweet singer with harp half-hid

who speaks with the cry of cicadas

who tells the tale too truly

for the ones with no one to tell them

the true tale of sound and fury

the Jack of Hearts who lays it out

who tells it as it is

the one who wears no watch

yet tells the time too truly

and reads the Knight of Cups

and knows himself

the Knave of Hearts the Jack of Hearts

who stole the tarts

of love & laughter

the Jack who tells his dream

to those with no one to dream it

the one who tells his dream

to the hard-eyed innocents

and lays it out for the blind hippie

the black dream the white dream

of the Jack of Hearts

whose skeleton is neither black nor white

the long dream the dream of heads & hearts

the trip of hearts the flip of hearts

that turns the Hanged Man right side up

and saves the Drowned Sailor

with the breath of love

the wet dream the hard dream the sweet dream

of the Deck Hand on the tall ship sailing softly

Blackjack yellowjack the steeplejack

who sets the clock in the tower

and sees the chimes of freedom flashing

his only watch within him

the high one the turned-on one the tuned-in one

the one who digs

in the time of the ostrich

and finds the sun-stone

of himself

the woman-man

the whole man

who holds all worlds together

when all is said and all is done

in the wild eye the wide eye

of the Jack of Hearts

who stands in a doorway

clothed in sun

Jeff Friedman **Dylan is God**

Dylan is God. You want proof?

Look at his scruffy beard, tormented eyes,

scarred hands healed after centuries,

his stomach still a little bloated

from his time on the cross.

Look how the goyim

follow him everywhere.

Even birds copy his songs,

singing from sturdy branches.

His words raise snakes up from the dust.

Satan buys all his CDs

and plays them for friends.

God writes his own songs and prayers

so people won't misquote him.

Money and fame are vanities, he claims.

All night women bang against

his four-posted bed, looking for salvation.

He's a tiger, he's a lamb.

He writes, "Jesus strangled Moses

for matzah. And me I scattered the hoses

and went into a wilderness of roses."

Once he came back as a duck,

quacking in Hebrew, davening

on High holidays, leading the children

out on the water. Once

he swallowed fire in a tent

and exhaled gold coins

and watched the audience tear itself apart.

Joan Baez says, God's a prick—

what does she know?

She's still singing his songs.

David Gaines **Egyptian Rings and Spanish Boots**

At first it was just about his words that contained multitudes.

Lyrics about things in the wind

And changing times.

Getting stoned and

Being directionless.

Not getting excited.

Then it was about finding others.

Tribe members who shared the code,

Fellow travelers who could not go three days without dropping one of his lines into our

conversations, long and winding, short and sweet, and so many places in between.

Or a season without striving for one of his looks:

Hair by Glaser and scarf of *Blonde on Blonde*,

Rolling Thunder feathered hat and Indian blanket jacket,

Egyptian rings and Spanish boots.

Finally, it returned to his oceans of language.

The stuff of our pillow talk and phone conversations,

Of those moments when

Crickets do talk back and forth in rhyme and the sun does sink like a ship.

And, most of all, of the enormous worlds within his phrase

Most of the time...

Cecilia Gigliotti **Arlo Guthrie Remembers Bob Dylan**

The guy on our doorstep

that cold day in 1960

was calling my dad his hero.

I thought, *you're not the first*.

I was twelve and just smart enough

to realize I wasn't looking in a mirror—

it was the curl in his hair that did it—

but that could be me

ten years from now,

or my dad

twenty-five years in reverse.

I saw the boots,

the hat,

the jacket,

and I didn't know whether to laugh or hit him.

He had nothing to sell

and something you couldn't buy.

Nora came up behind me—

I could almost feel her

tugging at her braids—

and I couldn't articulate

the lightning sensation

before she closed the door.

The sitter said Nora was right,

we couldn't just let somebody in.

I gave my guitar the old eyeball,

thought about what he'd carried on his back.

When he came back,

I let him in,

and a few songs later

no one argued.

Allen Ginsberg **Postcard to D----**

Chugging along in an old open bus

    past the green sugarfields

      down a dusty dirt road

        overlooking the ocean in Fuji,

thinking of your big Macdougal Street house

    & the old orange peels

      in your mail-garbage load,

        smoggy windows you clean with a squeejee

          3 March 1972

Benjamin Goluboff **"Bob Dylan and Entourage, 1964"**
by Daniel Kramer. Gelatin Silver Print.

Kramer traveled with Dylan
for a year and a day
as '64 became '65.
Shot him playing pool in Kingston,
chess at Woodstock,
and backstage in New Brunswick, N.J.,
where he posed,
a slim ironic bride,
in the arms of Johnny Cash.

Here Kramer takes him
in the dressing room
of Princeton's McCarter Theater
with Allen Ginsberg, Peter Orlovsky,
and Barbara Rubin.
Kramer frames them
in the dressing room mirror,
and what we see are their reflections.
Kramer himself stands
back in the right corner,
almost out of the frame,
his face mostly obscured
by the camera.

Orlovsky, long and elegant,
leans in the other corner,
dissembling boredom.
Rubin stands at the center
of the composition
not even bothering to dissemble.
Dylan and Ginsberg
sit in the foreground,
talking to each other.

The picture's focal point
is not Ginsberg,
who is turned three-quarters
from the mirror,
his bald spot exposed,
his face largely unseen.
And it is not Dylan,
who wears the harmonica holster,
holds a cigarette,
and seems to be speaking
on the exhale.
The focus of the composition
is a point on the line
between the two men's faces:
a line on which their words travel.

Ray Gonzalez **Bob Dylan in El Paso, 1963**

Bob Dylan passed through my hometown
to cross into Juarez, Mexico.

He used the Stanton Street bridge that
arched over the river and led to the red lights.

When he sang, "They got some hungry
women there and they'll really make a mess

out of you," my buddies and I knew the place,
the high school ritual of having to go there

to find Dylan and his shadow going upstairs.
Dylan must have had breakfast somewhere

in El Paso because you could never cross
without a good set of huevos and tortillas

churning inside you, ready to explode in
the sunrise colors of a frontier dream.

Dylan sang, "When you're lost in the rain
in Juarez and it's Easter time, too"

and I searched for the mission where
he might have knelt and prayed, entered

to find statues of saints draped in dark
colors like a waiting concert stage.

It didn't matter he was Jewish, because
all men going to the Juarez night

have to kneel and pray sometime.
Dylan sang, "I started out on burgundy,

but soon hit the harder stuff," and
I bought a bottle of mescal in Juarez

for him, the worm at the bottom of
the round jar still there after 45 years,

the black liquid churning dreams Dylan
had when he entered The Cave, the name

of the legendary cantina etched on
the tamale leaves Dylan left on his plate.

Bob Dylan passed through my hometown
after he left Juarez, Mexico.

His shadow is still there, appearing every
now and then in profile on the mountain

surrounding the town, the only El Pasoans
who know it is him growing fewer in number

because the silver raven has taken many of
them away, though there is a rumor

The Cave is still open for business,
the women waiting, the most popular

bedroom half paradise-half museum
because one of the dirty, adobe walls has

writing in faded lipstick that says,
"Zimmerman Was Here."

Juliana Gray **The Last Time I Saw Dylan**

He looked like Vincent Price: black
suit, pencil mustache, his voice
a raven's croak. If he still loved
performing, he kept it secret, blowing
his harmonica with his back turned
to the audience. He sounded awful,

really, and I expected awful.
His white hat cast wings of black
across his eyes as he slowly turned
to the piano and dragged his voice
through "Simple Twist of Fate," blowing
the lyrics, wrecking the song I loved.

Inheriting my father's love
for Dylan, I grew up full of awe
of every holy note of "Blowin'
in the Wind." The pristine black
vinyl of Dad's collection turned,
and we'd listen together to that voice.

Even then, Dylan's voice

wasn't pretty, but I learned to love

the rasps and burrs, the way he turned

not just love but pain, an awful

lonesomeness, to pure black

lines of poetry, blowing

like the western wind, blowing

an idiot wind. My father's voice

when I called about the show was black

with envy—he said he would have loved

to see the concert with me, awful

as it was. The years have turned.

My father is dead, and Dylan's turned

out another album, blowing

the critics away. How sad and awful

to hear those songs, that voice

and not the other voice I loved,

burned away to ashes black.

If he returned, he would have loved

the Duquesne whistle's blowing, the voice

an awful mourner's rag of black.

George Green **Bangladesh**

We have to start in 1965,

when all the gay meth heads couldn't decide

which one they most adored, Callas or Dylan,

both of them skinny as thermometers,

posing like sylphs in tight black turtlenecks.

Then, gradually, a multitude of Dylans

began to fill the park, croaking like frogs,

strumming guitars, blowing harmonicas

hundreds and hundreds, several to a bench.

But there was only one Maria Callas,

sequestered in her gloomy Paris pad

and listening to Maria Callas records

(and nothing but), her bulky curtains closed,

which works for me because it worked for her.

What doesn't work is three David Lee Roths,

one checking bags at *Trash and Vaudeville,* one

strutting with ratted hair up St. Mark's Place,

and one zonked out in tights and on the nod,

surrounded by the Dylans in the park.

David Lee Roth times three would mean the times

would have to change, and so a roving band

of punk rockers began to beat the Dylans,

chasing them through the park and pounding them

senseless, then busting up their folk guitars

or stealing them. They even torture one

unlucky Dylan by the children's pool,

holding him down to burn him with Bic lighters,

then cackling when he begs to keep his Martin.

Later on at the precinct, deeply troubled,

a sensitive policeman contemplates

the crimes. Why were marauding gangs of punks

beating the Dylans in the park? He asks

himself, repeatedly, not realizing

that they, the punks, were cultural police

determined to eradicate the Dylans

and purify the park of Dylanesque

pollutions and corruptions, rank and abject

folk rock recrudescences, and worse—

that odious and putrid piety,

the sanctimoniousness of all the Dylans,

the phony holiness that peaks for Bob

(his faddish Christianity aside)

during the benefit for Bangladesh,

where George insists that Yoko not perform

and John agrees 'till Yoko blows her stack,

and they start primal-screaming at each other,

John flying out of JFK and nodding,

and Eric flying into JFK

and nodding. Well, Ravi would go on first,

the one and only Ravi Shankar, folks,

I saw him five times, three times high on acid,

the first time straight with Richard and his mom,

Debbie, who drove us down from Podunk High

to see him at the Syria Mosque (long gone,

bulldozed in '75). Debbie's not well.

Last August she was totally Alzheimered

and, my sweet lord, she made a pass at me,

which was embarrassing. Rebuffed but proud

she sat down on the porch swing with a thump,

and, chirping like a parakeet, she swung.

Jeff Gundy **Autobiography with *Blonde on Blonde***

The ragman drew circles on everything, but St. John dragged
his feet through them all, saying *In the beginning was the Word!*

until time shuddered like a bus with bad brakes and my dad
rubbed his face and sat down at the kitchen table, his farmer tan

glowing. It had been a windy day, and the brutal stench
of Hillman's hogs wafted through the screens. I whacked Kathy

on the back of the head just to hear her howl. It worked.
Then they drove me off to college, where I learned

that the not-yet has already happened, if you squint at it
just right. *I am, I said,* said Neil Diamond, and we had

to agree with that. Then the president explained that those
unwilling to kill for peace might once have been good people,

but godless communist drugs had made them into trolls
and orcs. We knew he was an idiot—we were elves and hobbits—

and decided to set off for Mordor to destroy the Ring

right after dinner. But somebody put on *Blonde on Blonde* again,

and it was just like the night to play tricks, and we could hardly

root out the fascist pigs while Louise and her lover were so entwined.

We walked down beside the dam instead, tried to lose ourselves

in the scant woods. I never got to Memphis or to Mobile.

The hard rain was already falling, but the sun still shone like glory

some of those afternoons, with classes over and the long night ahead

and water roaring down the spillway like the great I AM.

Margaret Hasse **Summer of Love, 1967**

Some men she picked up at a rally

or rock concert called her Earth Mother.

She'd be wearing a peasant blouse

and he'd have a peace sign on his T-shirt,

torn jeans pinned at the zipper.

His mouth tasted of garlic hummus.

Her perfume was patchouli oil.

On his *Nashville Skyline* album,

Dylan kept singing *Lay, Lady, lay,*

lay across my big brass bed.

A lover with magical powers

taught her positions she'd never

heard of until *The Joy of Sex*.

Sometimes they made love

in an apartment with beaded curtains,

candles in Chianti bottles.

Or on a yoga mat where mung beans

in the kitchen were beginning to sprout.

Once in a hammock and once, just once

in a big brass bed.

Michael Hettich **Nature Poem**

(for Bob Dylan)

I'm wondering how to fill it, that sack you left me
of sky, redundant as an egg...

—Bill Berkson

Something like a swarm of bees inside the air,
something like a mattress full of quills, or a tee-shirt
glistening with fish scales sloughed from the body
of a man who blistered his fingers on the clouds
he leaped to grab onto, as though he could become them,
so he could be rainfall. This is the grief
of wool hats in the tropics, or a bone in the river,
that's been smoothed into a pebble. You pick it up and wonder
what the wind might intend as it worries the trees—

but wind intends nothing, of course, like that pebble
falling through the ocean inside you, behind your
rib bones and moon-bone and closets full of blaring
ambulance-street-cars and broken fire trucks
hoping to rescue the snakes from your shoes
before they start sliding up your legs like vines
to poke into your holes. So I lean to read your palm,

close enough to smell that perfume you've sprayed

        on your clothes and hair as though that might make you

                less mortal. And it does, at least while the fevers

        are rising inside us and our fingers are stroking

that fur; at least while our barefoot dances

        continue long after the music's gone limp

                and the rain has reminded us again of the silence

        always inside, like the lake we dive into,

so crowded with the arm-length ravenous fish

        we think of as *sheriffs of the ocean*, though

                they're caught here in fresh water, sluggish with thirst

        and yearning for salt. But we let them devour us

anyway, the way a man might turn into

        the cat he petted, and purr his way into

                oblivion while his wife sat at home

        watching old sitcoms and picking at her fingernails

until they were bleeding, then doing pushups

        until she broke down and cried out   *dirt*

               will be dirt.   Remember: those fish weren't fooled

        by the flies you tied with your father, leaning

in the near-dark basement workroom, while

your mother took her clothes off in the kitchen upstairs,

lay down on the floor and dreamed she might melt

into a skeleton to demonstrate just how

a fish might shiver. And soon there was glittering

glass in the path you walked, barefoot,

thinking you might still escape the relentless

dogs in your body—large dogs that howled

like wolves and were always ravenous, until

your bare feet left blood prints all over the floor

beside your mother, while your father took a shower

and sang in the voice of Ella Fitzgerald

or Bessie Smith, if they could have sung

like a man who sang like a woman, off key,

and the walls started sweating as the rain seeped through

the wallpaper your mother had hung, pictures

of fruits that have never existed, and carrots,

interspersed with small mammals—bunnies and squirrels—

cute creatures, while off in the distance the farmhouse

waited so patiently it almost made you cry

as the horses and pigs there exploded, one by one.

Tony Hoagland **Hard Rain**

After I heard "It's a Hard Rain's Gonna Fall"

played softly by an accordion quartet

through the ceiling speakers at the Springdale Shopping Mall,

then I understood: there's nothing

we can't pluck the stinger from,

nothing we can't turn into a soft drink flavor or a T-shirt.

Even serenity can become something horrible

if you make a commercial about it

using smiling, white-haired people

quoting Thoreau to sell retirement homes

in the Everglades, where the swamp has been

drained and bulldozed into a nineteen hole golf course

with electrified alligator barriers.

You can't keep beating yourself up, Billy

I heard the therapist say on television

                                        to the teenage murderer,

About all those people you killed—

You just have to be the best person you can be,

                                one day at a time—

and everybody in the audience claps and weeps a little,

because the level of deep feeling has been touched,

and they want to believe

that the power of Forgiveness is greater

than the power of Consequence, or History.

Dear Abby:

My father is a businessman who travels.

Each time he returns from one of his trips,

his shoes and trousers

                                        are covered with blood but

he never forgets to bring me a nice present;

Should I say something?

                            Signed, America.

I used to think I was not part of this,

that I could mind my own business and get along,

but that was just another song

that had been taught to me since birth—

whose words I was humming under my breath,

as I was walking through the Springdale Mall.

Holly Iglesias **Plaza San Miguel**

Across the way my past sips coffee, her cup, like mine, steaming. She is dressed like the girl who belongs to Bob, the one who never stumbles, the one who's got no place to fall, and I like the woman in a red pashmina with everything she needs to start looking back. We sit, silent, as the Spanish of Spaniards fills the square, as she jots in a notebook a beggar's plea, the whisper of lovers, as I pray she'll look up and see me. But she refuses. There is no comforting her now, far from home, convinced that exile is an act of will, determined to sharpen the dull contours of youth.

Lowell Jaeger **The Great Bob Dylan Debate**

It makes no sense, my older brother said.
The words make no sense. We shared
a bedroom through junior high, and kept
a little radio on the nightstand between us.

Turn it down, Dad commanded from the dark
of our parents' bedroom too nearby. I'd waited
to hear this particular song, and now I strained
and leaned closer. *Shhh*, I said to my brother.

The words make no sense, he said again.
Then I made a big mistake; I tried to explicate
Dylan's lyrics, as my brother raised his eyebrows,
smirked, and cocked his head sideways.

Got tangled up in my efforts to untangle.
So I talked on and on, more loudly,
twisting the song to make sense. Dad hollered,
Turn that damn thing off and both of you hush.

My brother's face filled with glee to see me stumble

as I whispered, and strained to convince him,

and I wanted to punch him because he was right.

I hated the hiss of my insistent half-baked analysis.

And I hated my brother for long afterwards,

though really he'd done me a great favor.

I was hearing something the words weren't saying,

something in the spaces between. Poetry

is what I'd call it now all these years after. Back then

I couldn't make sense of how words

can't always hold what the heart sings clearly.

And feelings aren't easy to explain.

Diane Jarvenpa **Bob Dylan Songbook**

When I was thirteen
I shoved you
in my backpack,
orange peels and tattered books
rubbed you with their oils.

I tore my skin,
fingers on frets
to fashion a rope,
the song I set my teeth into
to climb out of the window.

Shy feet
found hawk wings,
friends did not
believe my dreams,
but ballads defined me
in plain keys of D.

And I sang your songs
on hard church pews,
for the ghosts along
the Mississippi,
sitting on a milk crate
behind the pizza joint.

This was finding neon
inside hard rain,
your sling-shot words
shaped like a Fender,
a Siamese cat and myth.

The ragged pages sounded out
coyote call, quarter note
crooked highways,
messages to decode
and repeat ten times.
And this was my way out,
the songs of you
and the small dove voice of me
counting one, two, three, four—
and splitting up that wishbone.

Melissa Fite Johnson **Freewheelin' Bob Dylan
and the Nameless Girl**

I used to rifle through my mom's records,
basement floor, until I found this one. This was love,

Dylan in the thin jacket trying not to look cold,
the girl bundled in a trench, pressed against him.

In his memoir: *erotic, fair-skinned, golden-haired;*
the air suddenly filled with banana leaves.

The girl in the photo, seventeen, would be
Dylan's girlfriend for three years. She smiles

but shivers. Dylan doesn't smile or hold her hand.
He considers only the snow-covered street.

She died at sixty-seven, lung cancer, married
to Enzo Bartoccioli forty-four years. I search online,

Bartoccioli and Suze Rotolo, try to find their photos—
clearly *this* was love—but she's trapped in the sixties

at seventeen. She walks on Dylan's arm,
lights his cigarette, sprawls across their bed.

In her memoir: *Dylan was an elephant in the room*
of my life; I was a string on his guitar.

Andrew Jones **The Intro to Literature Professor's 115th Dream**

8AM: A musty Catholic college classroom.

"Where Are You Going, Where Have You Been?"

I offer to the silence, "Let's start with the dedication,"

queue up "It's All Over Now, Baby Blue," press play,

and close my eyes: Dylan slants behind the lectern—

some Flannery O'Connor misfit or Arnold Friend

in the flesh, sneering and foreboding like the pied piper

of the footnotes, a vagabond who doesn't need a gun,

just surly asides, just hijacked syntax

that rocks and shakes these kids awake,

that tells them where it's at, where they're going,

and prepares them for the second coming of Bob.

Nalini Jones **A Few Quick Words**

The night we met

you made your hand

a loose limp nest.

My name,

a less deliberate test.

Did either of us pass? But the joke was

gentled in your eyes;

a warm surprise, the kindness

kindling there.

We agreed I do not resemble my father.

That much was spoken. But before

our gaze was

broken, agreed as well that

even a moment, paper-

thin, can catch and flare

if held to flame,

lit bright before it chars

and curls,

puckish, precise,

absurd.

A dead-fish grip, a few quick words,

A twist of song, your quick hello.

George Kalamaras **Bob Dylan and
Julio Cortázar
Listen for the Rain
in an Outdoor Café
in Kentucky**

Bob Dylan is at an outdoor café in Kentucky, resting before the show. Somehow, Julio Cortázar is alive again, sitting with him, his beloved black cat licking one raised paw at the table in a seat between them. Dylan is mumbling something from inside the deepest place in Cortázar. Recesses of green ash and pin oak, shadblow serviceberries and sourwood. Cortázar, astounded at the way his own heartbeat sounds coming from the mouth of a blues harp. No, from a banjo tucked inside Dylan's spine. *This is hound dog country*, Dylan says, staring off into the Henry County hills. *We should all be so lucky. The merle-colored blueticks are starlight on four legs. Let me sing you a song of possum track in your chest. Here, Kitty, Kitty, come closer and rescue my mouth.* Cortázar is rewriting the *Iliad* as a sci-fi morality play, asking Bob who should play the giant alien plants paddling the slave ships, their leaf-shoots and vines wrapped around the oars. *War is war is lightning in the mouth of a blowfish near Shimonoseki*, says Dylan. *Afghanistan is Iraq is Syria is Sparta and the Peloponnese. All "Tangled Up in Blue." In the blue-green Sargasso Sea. On the other side of the world.* It is dusk. Here, in the Henry County hills. Afternoon has left. Rain seems far away. The sky tilting into the brief live mouths of mayflies. *I'm a coonhound man, Julio. Don't be so grave. You don't seem to be dead* now. *Come, get your Kafka on. Where's your Vallejo? Your Neruda and Miguel Hernández suit?* Cortázar is busy rewriting the entire Bible as just one of the 251 Hindu Upanishads. As a single hexagram of the I Ching. As chapter nine in the ninth book in the Hardy Boys Mystery Series. It all seems unknowable to the waiter, bringing the cat a bowl of fresh tuna mixed with milk. Listening in—as he does each trip to water the table—to the music pouring out of Cortázar's heart, up and out Dylan's mouth. *Not so loud*, Julio pleads. *I don't want the world to know the secret scars from my childhood stars. The way the pampas and jelly palms of Argentina worked their shade into me.* "It Ain't Me Babe," Dylan replies. And the Henry County hill hounds howl, as if Wendell Berry never walked the earth. His poem, "The Peace of Wild Things," only an idea. Unworded. Soon it will be time for the show. For the sound-check and side door. To bring some winter-part of Duluth into the warm places where coon hollers meet wind. Where Kentucky is Tennessee is Wichita Falls and a lightning-dark night in Fort Wayne, Indiana. *Here, Kitty, Kitty,* Dylan repeats, tapping the tabletop, then patting his lap, his mouth-harp voice trying to coax Cortázar's calm. *Come closer my furry heart. Let me hear your bobcat yowl. Rescue my mouth.*

Susan Doble Kaluza **On a Day Off, I Decide to YouTube Bob Dylan**

And his voice, its nasally rasp,

takes me back to my college dorm where I vowed my love

to his lips and their unstruck chords, their half-parted,

artful curve that defied description despite my nightly

wine drinking dances with adjectives

to land something solid between lovable and threatening.

Mostly it was his willful ignorance concerning his fame,

his not knowing what the fuss was about

that exuded such sexiness I bought the idea in life-sized posters

and gouged them into the plaster with silver thumbtacks.

When his eyes, in their gorgeous dumbfounded-ness,

broke through the aperture of my study lamp and tracked me

around the room, I'd crouch behind the armoire door

while brushing my teeth or changing my clothes.

I'd consider miserably how songs like "One more cup of coffee"

were written out of losses I could no more relate to than sing out of tune.

And yet I sang into the mirror with its dulled sheen

fixed resolutely beside the phone while I plucked my eyebrows

and narrowed my eyes as if to coax the exotic creature

I believed would commence from the few wisps I'd left intact,

as the yanked remains—each hair with its unbreakable double helix—

swam disembodied in the belly of the sink. Never once

had I considered life's losses in the form of my own follicles

swirling down the drain past the tear-shaped drip

that couldn't be scrubbed out even with hefty clumps of Ajax—

or think they'd eventually be missed

as I aged, while I rejoiced in mapping out my face,

even as I imagined it being touched, as my own eyes met

his whose unrelenting gaze followed me

through nine semesters, stalking me day and night

until I left the room.

Gerhard Kofler **Bob Dylan in Detroit**

Translated from the Italian and German by Geoff Howes

in the car once again to drive to Detroit

to finally hear Bob Dylan in concert too

after thirty-six years that had carved

this voice into you on flying discs

all around your mumbling from the bottom up

that sought song for itself in a certain sense

to go beyond it the way he also went

thirty-six years thus to be a river

and to find oneself in the sea under open sky

but open too for another war that's underway

to blow in the wind these roots of ours

out of fresh water in the salt of tears

vast horizon to recreate a cry

at the sight of all those lighters lighting

in a country that's even at war with smoke

BOB DYLAN A DETROIT

In macchina di nuovo per andare a Detroit
a sentire Bob Dylan finalmente in concerto
dopo trentasei anni che questa voce
ti è stata incisa sui dischi volanti
attorno al tuo mormorio di base
che il canto cercava in un certo senso
per andare oltre come pure lui ci andava
trentasei anni dunque per essere fiume
e trovarsi in un mare sotto cielo aperto
ma aperto pure per un'altra guerra in corso
per soffiare al vento le nostre radici
d'acqua dolce nel sale del pianto
orizzonte vasto per ricercare un grido
vedendo tutti quegli accendini accesi
in un paese in guerra anche con il fumo

BOB DYLAN IN DETROIT

im auto wieder um nach Detroit zu fahren

um zu hören bob dylan endlich im konzert auch

nach sechsunddreißig jahren in denen diese stimme

dir eingeritzt war auf fliegenden scheiben

rundherum um dein murmeln vom grund her

das den gesang auf eine gewisse art sich suchte

um darüber hinaus zu gehen so wie auch er ging

sechsunddreißig jahre um ein fluß zu sein also

und im meer sich zu finden unter offenem himmel

der aber auch offen für einen krieg der wieder in gang ist

um in den wind zu blasen unsere wurzeln

aus süßwasser da im salz der tränen

weiter horizont um den schrei neu zu schaffen

beim anblick all der feuerzeuge die angezündet

in einem land das auch mit dem rauch im krieg ist

Yusef Komunyakaa **Gift Horse**

Your wife's forty-five

today & you've promised her

someone like me, did I

hear you right? You

wave a hundred-dollar bill

under my nose & a diamond

of snowlight falls through

the bar's isinglass walls

as Dylan comes up on the jukebox.

You saw me hustling pool tables

for nickels & dimes, now my refusal

rocks you like a rabbit punch

in the solar plexus. You pull

snapshots from your wallet.

Yeah, she does look like

Shirley Jones in *Elmer Gantry.*

You say you're a man

who loves the truth,

& maybe my mistake is

I believe you.

I know the dark oath

flesh makes with earth.

You drive a hard bargain

for a stone to rest your head on.

On the jukebox, Otis Redding's "Dock of the Bay."

Days fall around us

bigger than the snowstorm

that drove you in here

to dodge wind driving pine needles

through the hearts of birds.

You up the ante another fifty.

My bottle of beer sweats

a cool skin for us both.

You blow smoke-ring halos

for dust-colored angels among tinsel,

reindeer & year-round Christmas lights,

where sexual hunger's like ripe apples,

but by now you must know I can't

sleep in your bed while you drive

around the countryside till

sunrise, taking the blind

curves on two wheels.

Norbert Krapf **Arlo and Bob Go Fishing**

Arlo, whose daddy Woody brought home some big ones, was once talking to Bob. "Hey, Bob," he tells us he said, "why don't you throw some little ones back in?" Arlo makes it sound like there was a pause, a big heavy one, between what he asked and what he hoped Bob might say. We all knew what Arlo was thinking. Here's a guy like Bob, a little slip of a thing, standing on the bank of the river throwing his line in and nonchalantly pulling in these big ones, one after another. Doesn't seem fair. We can see Arlo and other songwriters standing downstream from Bob, waiting for a nibble, praying to hook even a little silver minnow of a song while Bob's pole keeps bending over double. "Yeah, Bob," we're all thinking, "why don't you be nice and throw some of the little ones back in so we can catch something, anything!"

But Bob doesn't bite. I mean he doesn't go for the bait. Bob is one serious, determined, no-nonsense fisherman. Fishing for song is a matter of life and death. No jokes allowed. We all get this, looking up at Arlo from our seats. We're all little guys, throwing our lines into the waters that can be swift or slow, shallow or deep, clear or murky, sunlit or shadow-laden. We're all little guys willing to settle for any catch. We ain't greedy. We want to leave something for the future. We all got mouths to feed, but we know that the other guy's got to eat, too. We'll settle for anything that rises to the bait. And we think it's hilarious that Bob doesn't see how funny this is. Big-fish Bob won't even grin. "Come on, man," Arlo says in that twangy hip argot of speaking he must have inherited from his old man, "cancha throw a few little ones back in so's the rest of us can catch somethin'?" Yeah, Bob, ain't you already caught enough big ones for one lifetime? Isn't there a season limit and a fine for going over it? How's come you gotta be greedy? How could such a little man pull in so many huge songs? What's your trick? What's your secret? Who taught you how to bait the hook and where to drop it into the water?

Makes you wonder if maybe old Woody didn't take Arlo fishing at least a few times and tell his little boy some big ones about the fish that did NOT get away. Like the time he dangled his cane pole in the water and pulled up that monster from the deep, the one whose chorus begins, "This land is your land." Imagine that, pulling in a whole land, a whole country and its people, a whole continent into a single song. Your daddy tells you a tale like that and for the rest of your life you can't help but wonder when the big one's gonna strike. Poor little Arlo. Maybe that's why Bob didn't laugh. Bob held his tongue. He understood.

Dorianne Laux **Bob Dylan**

Father of minutes, father of days...

I was born without a father, born again
without another. I searched the grassy
corridors of childhood, calling his name.
Only the birds called back, then returned
to ordering their feathers, dipping their beaks
in muddy gutter water. If I kill an ant
I kill it dead. I don't want anything to suffer.
Once I brushed a stinging column of them
from my dress. I got down on my knees,
watched how one, without a leg, limped
in circles, sent two front legs out to stroke
a crooked antennae, a gesture that looked
too much to me like prayer. I knew
it wasn't true. I knew there was no mercy
but me. Even at that young age
the great questions had been set down.
An empty plate. So I went on without,
like everyone else. Calling, calling.
That's what the old man is doing now,
sleeping under a bare tree in the park,
his sack of clothes beneath his matted head.
He's twitching in dream. One hand clutching
the bald earth, the other waving me down.

Jim LaVilla-Havelin **September 1980/
More Than His City**

went into the city to read

baseball poems at The Public Theatre

and they put us up in The Chelsea Hotel

guess what I was humming when we checked in

when we walked down the hall

sitting in the lobby, nervous about the reading

"staying up for nights in the Chelsea Hotel,

writing 'Sad-Eyed Lady of the Lowlands' for you"

and then slowly switching from

"Sara, Sara"

to "sad-eyed-lady-don't-you weep"

in an almost drone-voiced memory

but there were Warhol's rooms and stories

and Leonard Cohen, and I walked out onto 23rd Street,

a fire engine clanged by, siren howling—for

Demuth and Williams

and there was Frank O'Hara saluting Mayakovsky

and the sun, Crane's bridge, and the street scenes of

Walker Evans and Helen Levitt

went into the city

and his songs wrapped around street corners

and subway stops, guitar strumming street musicians

and all-night diners

city of stories, of songs, Whitman and Ginsberg,

of Langston, Charlie Parker, Birdland and The Apollo,

Basquiat, Rollins on the bridge, The Strand, *The Voice*

echoes the halls of The Chelsea Hotel

more than his city, but rolled in from Minnesota

with a guitar slung on his back

and claimed it.

Richard Levine **Animation Hero**

I once saw Bob Dylan in concert.
He was old and about three inches tall.
His songs seemed longer, but no longer
his. Still good, though, even without
the arrogance. The band, too, could have turned up
and been dismissed even in a dive bar.
They were that anonymous.

Dylan played piano standing up. In his green
western suit and hat, he was a comic commix
of Hank Williams and the animation hero in *Toy Story.*

His voice and the moon were slivers,
and every word sounded thrust through a sneer.
Defying time and space, he repainted
a few of his six-string masterpieces in keyboard chords.
We didn't recognize them at first. Some people gestured and jeered.

It was like they wanted to hear
"The Times They Are A-Changin'" without changes,
like they wanted to forget people were still in the streets
begging for the same changes, like they wanted the song
to make them young and beautiful and hopeful, again.

Dylan, not at all animated, played on.

M. L. Liebler **John Lennon Comes Back to New York City to Pay Homage to Bob Dylan**

He comes back

A little pale, but no worse

For the wear and tear of being

Away, in another dimension,

For some twelve odd years. Now,

He knows everything

Is off the record. Things have changed

A lot and a little since he left

In early December 1980.

But he doesn't think in those terms

Anymore. Where he's been there is

No time, no dates to remember, no

Appointments to keep, no

Memory of a past or a present

At all. He pauses, for what to some might seem

A minute or two, on a city corner. He thinks

To himself that *he hasn't thought*

To himself in a long, long time,

And he knows there is now no concern

About measurements. No dates—no time—no years.

These things used to cause him pain. The future

Is always happening for him.

So, once again, he finds himself

In New York City, beloved home

Away from home. City

Where he has always felt

Comfortable and safe. If a person could see

Him now and approach him, gently,

And if that person were to suggest murder,

He wouldn't understand, nor would he

Consider the idea. He would swiftly dismiss

It, as quickly as waving away the vague

Street clouds rising from city grids.

Lennon glances up to see

A sign, lights flashing

Through a crowd. He recognizes

A building. He thinks he has been

There before. He sees, but he can't

Be seen. He likes that. It fits

His style—both, then and now. He checks

Around for a street name to remember

Where he might be. He believes

He knows where he is.

He smiles. He overhears people

Talking about Bob Dylan, and something

Seems to be going on here, but he "Doesn't know

What it is." He chuckles to himself. He is

The thin man. Everyone has come

To pay homage, to sing songs,

To celebrate old friends, and he too

Wants to pay his respect because he and Bob

Go way back to England days. Before Dylan

Was as he later became. Before electric

Guitar mania at Newport, before motorcycle nightmares,

Before guru love, before Berkeley in the 60s, before

There ever was a Sgt. Pepper. Before . . . He thinks

About a young Bobby Zimmerman riding

In the back of a rented Bentley, joking

Through the streets of London, a mighty long way

From Hibbing and Duluth. Dylan poking

Fun at American folk-a-rockers, et al.

Lennon is stoned, and Dylan, too, is way gone,

With a small movie camera running, capturing them

And Dylan wants to make a film

Called *Eat This Document*. Lennon doesn't

Want any part of this madness. Now,

Even now, he knows much crazy madness

Will come: Vietnam, various arrests, miscarriages, police

badgering, Yoko's love, lost weekends.

He has already been

On Ed Sullivan at this point, and

He doesn't want to deal with a babbling, drunk

Bob Dylan, so he giggles nervously, and hopes

The camera will run itself

Out. He doesn't care if years later

Beatle fan-at-tics will see

Bootleg videos of him and Dylan stoned,

but he doesn't want to hurt the feelings

Of Barry McGuire, Johnny Cash. He decides

To let Dylan worry

About pulling his own foot out

Of his own mouth. In years to come,

When Dylan finally meets Johnny Cash, he will

Make a record along a *Nashville Skyline*. Lennon knows

This, and he further knows he won't be around

Much more than another 15 years. Still,

He recognizes greatness, and he realizes,

While sitting in the backseat, that there will be

A tribute, someday, to his old friend. Down

The road people will celebrate this skinny kid

With puffy, punky big hair and nasal

Twang. He's right!

Everyone has come. Tonight is very special,

And Lennon just happens to be

Back in New York City for a while.

He notices many people while wandering

Around backstage. In the distance

He sees a familiar face,

A stagehand who once got him

A guitar chord when he was so nervous

And so stiff and so afraid before

His 1972 benefit concert at The Garden.

Seeing this stagehand's familiar face seems to excite Lennon

In many ways more than seeing any

Of his old pop star friends

Behind the action, behind the music, there he is still

Doing his stagehand job, just as if twenty years had not

Passed. When Lennon turns his head, he is

Sitting in the tenth row-center, next to

a young lady who is the wife of a midtown business man.

She lives, happily, in Fort Lee, New Jersey, but tonight

her soul belongs to Dylan and to Manhattan. She has

Always loved Dylan. She remembers seeing him

Many times ever since his early 60s start

In The Village. As the lady contemplates her past,

Boos and bad spirits erupt and fly

Out like millions of dark sparrows. Lennon is confused.

He looks up to the ceiling and quickly to the stage.

He notices a bald-headed woman in the spotlight.

In an instant he realizes

She is the one feeding these birds. People whisper

Something about her inappropriate behavior

On national television. Lennon knows all about this.

He has made a similar gaffe, several years ago.

He hardly ever uses memory this way anymore.

But he can't help but recall a teen mag interview

And a statement he made

By mistake. It cost him

What the bald headed singer must pay

For herself. She is forced to run off

The stage in tears. He knows, all too well,

That kind of pain and its hurtful consequences.

It feels like he and Yoko

All over again, and he hates that evil

Feeling, but it has been a long time

Now, and all the time is off the record.

His attention is, again, diverted.

He now finds himself in the cheap back

Balcony seats. He remembers Aunt Mimi, Liverpool,

Strawberry Field, Julia, briefly in this moment, he remembers

The concert halls of late 1950s Britain,

And the best he could ever afford

Were the cheap-cheap, faraway, back seats. Four guys

Seated nearby mention Eric Clapton's name, and Lennon

remembers

One late summer night in Toronto, Canada. He,

On stage with long, long hair, dark full beard

Holding beautiful Yoko while young, wired

"Slowhand" plays Holy Rock'N'Roll.

The crowd grows

Pleasantly still and they gasp.

Lennon sits

Stage left; he is attentive. He now senses loneliness

For the first time in a long time. He

Suddenly realizes this is why

He came here tonight. There,

In a purple jacket, is a youthful long-hair

With cherished, cherub smile. George

Harrison. Old dharma buddy who had made the journey

With John from Liddypool to Hamburg in 1962.

New Year's Decca audition

to the "toppermost of the poppermost" to America

To India to NYC, where Lennon's drained blood

Would evaporate outside

72nd Street and Central Park West,

To forever. Tonight, young George is his wonderful

Friend. Lennon wants to tell George

Where he has been all these years,

But he doesn't know

Where to begin anymore.

Lennon wants to climb up

Onto the stage and sing

In old harmony spirit, but

Tonight is for George to repay his debt

To Bob Dylan for coming to George's aid

To help an old friend from Bangladesh to

Save his country, and Lennon stops

To meditate on the silly reasons why he refused

To show that night to honor

His English brother's request.

He remembers those different times

And those hard, different feelings

And they are all so difficult

To imagine anymore. George passionately sings.

Tonight his voice is like silk and honey

For Lennon's dreamy heart. It is

At this point that Lennon decides

Not to visit anyone else

Tonight. He thinks it is best to walk away

And to love time for what it was.

He wants to keep it all

Framed just that way. He is very happy

To see George up there shining

On and on. He is very pleased and fully satisfied.

He thinks that perhaps he might cry,

But he knows there are no more tears,

And, besides, nobody will ever know

That on a cool night,

Through a mid-October wind,

John Lennon came back

To New York City to pay

His own kind of homage

To Bob Dylan.

Lyn Lifshin **Snow was Melting on My New**

abalone and onyx hoops.

Christmas vacation with

my Syracuse boyfriend.

Gerde's Folk City,

pizza and beer flowing.

I forget who the main singer

was when a chubby

guy got up to sing in

baggy clothes.

Half the audience turned

away, others giggled.

But there in my mini skirt

and spider medallion,

I thought this is different,

interesting. I like this

Robert Dylan.

Laurinda Lind **Conductor**

Jean Thompson used to write Dylan lyrics
in her notebook during classes at Plattsburgh,
dense blocks of stanzas in smartass handscript
forty years ago, doors that gave her exits
right out onto the tracks. I couldn't do that,
but I'm full of him anyway, we all were.
The enemy twin, the lover in the sewer,
the hard rain, the railroad gin. We couldn't
help it, he was there early, ore for allegory,
moody watchtower trickster who made
new faces and mouths for the same dark
wild mind. I was too young to ride that train,
even when it came slow. When I saw him
in Syracuse he walked out late and looked
haunted, wandered the stage, was barely
there. My friend Lori said he did the same
that summer in Denver, said he looked like
he'd been rode hard and put away wet, yet,
yet, yet, I saw him, I saw him, and still today
he is alive under the same sky. He didn't
have to be first or even best. He just had
to be the right live wire down the right
crack, and then the lightning could come.

Lachlan MacKinnon **Bob Dylan's Minnesota
Harmonica Sound**

Open-cast mining country, a hole so vast

the diggers looked as tippable as toys

if you stood on the rim and gazed across it;

iron for world wars, iron for Korea,

but thinning. Scraggly grass and mud, the light

grey as age in the early days of autumn,

when first frost prickled and the mountains shook

in the wind that seemed to be always blowing,

blowing and sucking. Shrunken forests,

spruce and fir, pines, moccasin country,

a map freckled with water, bogs absorbing

the blue-green needles of the tamarack.

The freight-train whistles blew and sucked. Their wail

hung in the steady and insistent gusts

like a come-hither fading with the dusk.

Night was indoors, the sound of parents' friends.

All you could be was family or elsewhere.

A boy lounged on the main drag.

He was pretending he was James Dean,

he was pretending he was Baudelaire.

Small wonder, then, if home became a spotlight,

as, blowing and sucking, you count the changes,

wearing a hood like a cowl to shut

out the sound of the everlasting wind

that blows from childhood, blows to suck you back.

There's no solace or ease now for the soul

that kicked the mine-dust from its heels. Sometimes

the one comfort is never standing still.

C. P. Mangel **Tarantula**

who wants to be noticed anyway? only you ...
dont say you didnt know I was there ...
—Bob Dylan, Tarantula

Transfixed by the shrunken heads inside a glass

box at the back of a long side room, I returned

to the Oxford museum several times that summer

of nineteen eighty, passing the dusty stuffed

dodos and birds with ivory beaks and bones

of small winged dinosaurs to see the neckless

wrinkled faces no larger than an egg

eyes and shriveled lips sewn tightly closed

lengths of charcoal hair, flared nostrils, sealed ears.

Twelve girls shared one shower and two cramped toilets

on the fourth floor and the only way to have

a hot shower was to climb the stairs before

sunrise and wash your hair while the others slept.

Back in my bedroom in the seventeenth century

fireplace suite, I stood before the stained

pedestal bowl in my white briefs to brush

my teeth and comb my hair, shadow my eyes

with sable powder, while the springs of the bed

behind the shared wall played their reveille.

What they were doing I wanted to do

wanted someone to love me the way my roommate's

boyfriend loved her, though she would have no use

for him after the end of our summer abroad

when she would go to law school and meet polished

boys there called *Mister* by professors in class.

From the window of my small room there was little

to see, only the slate roof of adjacent

Balliol College, its pipes, old chimneys prodding

the wet and gray underbelly of the sky.

He warmed us up with "Prufrock" and "Hollow Men"

not only reciting all the words from memory

but igniting us with diction bright as the strike

of a match against stone. This was an Eliot

I had never heard before. And then he began

Tarantula. He will recite the book by heart,

one of the older students told me, as she crouched

near his leather armchair in her ragged jeans

resting on her worn stiletto heels and watching

how his lips moved, how his starched white shirt shifted

as he transmuted the words, rhythms of Dylan

into language as metaphysical

intoxicating, exhilarating as Donne

Herbert and Vaughan. Not a book or page of notes

did Christopher Ricks use in his alchemy

only a pint of ale, its dark gold oiling

his voice which seemed not to pause for breath.

This was no "Blowin' in the Wind" but words

fired into the sheen of porcelain.

One morning near the end of my course I stood

over the half melon bowl brushing my teeth

and through the drawn curtains an unusual brightness

rinsed away darkness, illuminating

every detail, dust on the windowsill,

turquoise bottle of cologne, saucer and floral

teacup, bone plate with bitten currant scone,

soap at my temple, dribble of paste on my breast.

I gazed at the sky. He floated into my view

the man perched on the ledge of the neighboring roof

suddenly near and staring intently at me.

I yanked the stale woolen curtains across

the panes of glass, snuffing out all the light.

Up from my throat came the burning bile, erupting

plumes of putrid hope and sulfurous yearning.

Gary Margolis **Poem for My Daughter
and Not for Bob Dylan
Singing at Fifty**

I didn't know what to expect sitting

    in a crowd mostly my age. Would

the woman in front of me weep or the man

beside her stand and sway, singing to

    himself? I didn't know if anyone would

light a joint they had saved as if it were

a candle or how Dylan would stand up

    over time. Outside I hadn't been pushed

in line and inside didn't have to ask

a crasher to get out of my seat. I knew

    you would be too tired to think straight

in school the next day after staying up

that late. But my father never took me

    anywhere with my date, never saw me put

my hand, when the music started

on her blouse, on the small of her back,

    never saw me lean over to kiss her

in the half-dark when I didn't think

anyone was watching, when I couldn't

    tell what the singer sang or what his words

meant, when all I knew was what I felt.

Debra Marquart **Dylan's Lost Years**

Somewhere between Hibbing and New York, the red rust streets of the Iron Range and the shipping yards of the Atlantic, somewhere between Zimmerman and Dylan was a pit stop in Fargo, a Superman-in-the-phone-booth interlude, recalled by no one but the Danforth brothers, who hired the young musician, fresh in town with his beat-up six-string and his small-town twang, to play shake, rattle, and roll, to play good golly, along with Wayne on the keys and Dirk on the bass, two musical brothers whom you might still find playing the baby grand, happy hours at the southside Holiday Inn.

And if you slip the snifter a five, Wayne might talk between how high the moon, and embraceable you, about Dylan's lost years, about the Elvis sneer, the James Dean leather collar pulled tight around his neck, about the late-night motorcycle rides, kicking over the city's garbage cans, and how they finally had to let him go, seeing how he was more trouble than he was worth, and with everyone in full agreement that the new boy just could not sing.

Michael McClure **Ode**

(for Bob Dylan)

MY EYES ARE WIDE EXPLOSIONS

in the field of nowhere.

My pocketwatch burns air

and sprouts golden antlers.

I'm

the stand-in

for flaming stars;

my heart murmurs

are electric guitars

and

my hair

reflects in rainbows

and in aura glows

that radiate my brow.

The tinsel ice

does melt

beneath my feet—

my words are fleet—

and my songs

are an armada.

I see

the smiles of cherubs float

from the barranca.

The world with all its facets

is a whirling boat

of leopards and of mice

from which I hurl

the radiant dice

of my perceptions.

All conceptions

of boundaries

are lies!

Linda Back McKay **Bob Dylan, Shirley Temple, The Beatles and So Forth**

Bob Dylan gets into the car and I say, *Look, we're going*

out to lunch now, so why don't you come along? He says he can't

because his fans are everywhere and they never leave him alone.

I say, *It's okay, you'll be with us and they won't recognize you. Why,*

when you walked down our road just now, with the sun at your back,

my daughter thought you were Shirley Temple.

When the preposterous is the mundane,

we know we must be dreaming.

This freedom to sing with the Beatles

and fly above the telephone wires

is our god given right.

When I dream about Bob, Shirley, Ringo and so forth,

we know each other's wisdom. This is profound,

our gentle secret.

We all share the blood on which babies slide into the world.

Our blood beads and rolls under the knife, spurts

from a moth on the windshield, fills the undertaker's sink.

War after war proves we are no smarter than before.

Nor have we proven we can live alone.

My daughter crouches on the little porch off her bedroom.

Through binoculars she spies on the neighbors, the dog.

She examines people's faces and hopes for visitors.

Her power is great.

Bill Meissner **1959: Bob Dylan Hitchhikes On Highway 61 Somewhere Outside Hibbing, Minnesota**

He's dancing with the wind.

Though it might look like he's standing still,

he's always dancing with the tattered wind

that scrapes across the open iron ore pits.

Tonight on this roadside there are no cars,

no Buick 6 roaring past, leaving him behind, dust devils

circling around his black boots.

The night's so quiet he can almost hear

the stones in the ditch begin to hum.

So he thinks of pulling his guitar

from that battered black case and strumming it,

though he hasn't written a note yet.

    He imagines that first song:

    Mountains and seas, cannonballs and doves, aching notes

    and the sudden vacuum.

He'll write it some day, he has to believe that:

With Woody Guthrie's ghost standing over his shoulder,

he'll sit down at his typewriter, slide in a blank sheet and

search behind his sunglasses for the ragged poet,

then snap out a verse or maybe

sixty-one, about neon madmen and chief preachers and diplomats

riding chrome horses,

all of them crumbling like statues slammed by the

hammers of his notes,

about Ramona and Jane and Johanna and Sara,

each of them coming alive for a few minutes

until he crumples the paper in his fist.

     He remembers his old high school—

     his Tom Thumb classmates during the talent show,

     their boos dropping like lead weights from their

     lips to the hard floor.

     He thinks about the stage curtain they closed

     on him in the middle of a song, trying to suffocate him.

     Instead it gave him breath, made him

     play the piano even louder to keep away all that silence.

Tonight there are no cars,

no whirr of tires,

no red taillights fading like tired eyes.

He looks down the empty highway, that asphalt arrow

pointing toward the distant horizon, and he knows

his future is out there, always pulling farther and farther away

no matter how much he walks toward it, or stands still.

Just before dawn he thinks he hears the stars fading,

their last shimmer making a jingle-jangle tambourine sound.

He stands there in the first blinks of sunlight:

He's a silhouette, the first dark note

of a song that will play

for a hundred years.

Michael Mingo **The Fury of the Moment**

The final track, as delicate as dust

brushed from a hymnal cover, waltzes through

the speaker gaps: from past to present day,

from dying voice to fellow wayward souls.

I won't allow it—not the cymbals struck

beneath the mix, the lone piano notes

breaking through the atmosphere, the strain

in Dylan's contemplations, none of it—

to stir my eyes. (It's only hymnal dust,

I've told myself.) The lyrics disappear

the moment they are sung; the Master's hand

remains invisible. My heart is hard,

resistant to his chisel, his homilies.

What force to batter water from a stone,

to break its jagged surface. I'm immune
to these entreaties—all except the low,

buzzing harmonica, the instrument
of shaken speech. It rises, then it fails:

a prayer ignored a dozen times. It cries,
loud as a locust plague, before becoming

a cold embrace around my head. The sound
is now a storm: it chokes my breath and stings

my closing eyes. I won't accept the message.
I've told myself it's only hymnal dust.

Paul Muldoon **Bob Dylan at Princeton, November 2000**

We cluster at one end, one end of Dillon Gym.
"You know what, honey? We call that a homonym."

We cluster at one end, one end of Dillon Gym.
"If it's fruit you're after, you go out on a limb."

That last time in Princeton, that ornery degree,
those seventeen year locusts hanging off the trees.

That last time in Princeton, that ornery degree,
his absolute refusal to bend the knee.

His last time in Princeton, he wouldn't wear a hood.
Now he's dressed up as some sort of cowboy dude.

His last time in Princeton, he wouldn't wear a hood.
"You know what, honey? We call that disquietude.

It's that self-same impulse that has him rearrange
both 'The Times They Are A-Changin' and 'Things Have Changed'

so that everything seems to fall within his range
as the locusts lock in on grain silo and grange."

Katie Darby Mullins **Seeing Bob Dylan for the Second Time**

When I was thirteen, I had already learned

less popular records were cooler (thanks, Dad)—

and I spent a summer with *Self Portrait* on repeat,

studying the difference in Sadies and learning

how "Cocaine Blues" can morph in new time signatures.

That summer I learned the art of the cover: songs

sung in a new voice, the caterpillar turning himself

inside out to reveal the wings that were always

trapped inside its slinky body. How Dylan even learned

to cover himself, to sing "She Belongs To Me" in a new

voice. I wanted to learn to be like that, to grow

and open my mouth and have the same words mean

different things. I wanted to see him live, a pilgrimage,

and when he came to the Coca-Cola Starplex,

co-headlining with Paul Simon, my dad told me if

I washed his car, that would save him enough money

to buy tickets. And there I was, too young to really

understand how a simple twist of fate changes everything,

that those songs weren't just moments that spun

around on a 33, watching Dylan and Simon share

a microphone to sing "The Boxer," and I was crushed

under the weight of the places only ragged people go.

*

On my own, the fighter still remained: my parents

had long since divorced and remarried each other

when I went looking for a job and was hired

to review a live Bob Dylan concert. I'd long since

grown out of my interest in covers, long since

learned that you can't afford to see a show with money

you save on one car wash. Without my dad, this time

alone, I saddled up and went, knowing that this Dylan

would feel different now that it was his words, not

the nuance of the performance, that would reach me.

And maybe the years had not been kind to Dylan

with his trademark growl, but when he sang

I felt baptized in his declaration:

Beyond the horizon, at the end of the game

Every footstep you take, I'm walking the same

Beyond the horizon, the night winds blow

The theme of a melody from many moons ago

And for just a second, I was thirteen again,

covered in soap suds and car sludge, praying

to one day be someone who just *got* it, man,

just understood Dylan, like my dad, who

drank those songs in like water, who loved

Blood on the Tracks, who took me to the show

even when I could just barely articulate

that yes, this *means* something, this is real.

Eileen Myles **Bob Dylan**

(for Shannon Ebner)

I can't taste my pie

this mood goes elsewhere

past my dirty hands

Like a noodle to a spring

teeny weeny bites

I'm like a big yelp

ulp Hello

my lines look all wrong

if this is the way

I'm flung

into history

Here is my house.

Tim Nolan **Microfilm**

I crammed my head full of as much of this stuff as I could
stand and locked it away in my mind out of sight, let it alone.
—Bob Dylan, *Chronicles: Vol. 1*

At the New York Public Library, the lions preside over every day
whether the day begins in fog or sleet or a pile of snow.
In the microfilm cubby, on a wobbly table, he spun the film

through those shiny sprockets, paused on medicinal remedies,
the news from Fort Sumter, the call-up of recruits. The day
he was in didn't matter too much. He had slept in someone's apartment,

listened to records, read a French poet, drank coffee with sugar and cream.
The day that mattered was long ago. He was trying to hear the music
of that day through the news of that day, the songs they played at

Dodsworth's Dancing Academy in Brooklyn, the melody of Professor Wood's
Hair Restorative, the simple American sense of Winslow's Soothing Syrup,
for teething children, impressive testimonials. You never can know

what you might need, a phrase, a turn, an odd coincidence. The words
come into focus when you turn the black knob. The important thing—
to lock it away, let it alone, being certain it will all come back again.

Jeni Olin **Bob Dylan**

I'd screw the young Dylan in a headdress
Between flayed columns & evergreens
     Alphabetize lesions. Swelling

The meticulous, if tormented, transcription of a head
       But I've only been ahead so I guess
Trellised behind bean futures & nuclear

Fallout. London stoned. He's much about
     Interstices, different versions of haircut
The casting down as darling:

So "the blood just ran out" & he was left "scared again"

With brackish nausea
On the threshold of a bored game. Swelling
     With illustrations of people walking off

Shattered teens on facet planes. *Blood on the Tracks*
     Scored lightly. I said, I break
For strophes & isotopes. Dylan remains

Skeletal in studio light. Pan to face & dissolve—
"Are you sure there is an audience? I won't go if there's no audience . . ."
     "Everywhere I turn, arms burst their darks!"

Lisa Panepinto **No Direction Home**

my hands wind cracked

eyes heavy black

frozen expanse

rolling out of my head

into highway mist

it's hard to remember

where i come from

and where i go

rest stop private showers

and rows of white sinks

ask me what will you wash first

your hands face teeth

eyes clothes dishes hair

no women journeying

this road but me

they're making phone calls

writing letters

holding the world

together

the soil eroding

in treeless gray fields

the same moment

playing itself out

again and again

Native chants

on the fm dial

drums echoing from the fields

the only song that exists

coal blue devils lake

whitecaps and people

walking on the waves

two bodies bend over

to collect a fire

they pull fish from the shore

harvest beets from the fields

tall grass howling in the wind

where once there lived only

giant majestic white birds

i make a lasting fire under thousands of stars

it takes practice to be alive

expecting to ride off

the continent at any time

to where the sun comes from

after hundreds of miles of wounded fields

in willows and birch

i feel the gentleness of all the earth

Linda Pastan **Listening to Bob Dylan, 2006**

Little Bobby Zimmerman,
did he have a mother?
Iconoclast to icon,
was the wind his brother?

Did he steal or borrow
Woody's voice, pure gravel?
Women gave their bodies.
Kerouac gave travel.

Some would call him genius
or curly headed sphinx,
riding music out of sight
and noisy as a lynx.

Here we go again,
counting up our dead:
syncopated bullets,
hard rain on our heads,

foxes in the hen house,
freedom on the rack.
Somebody sing something!
The times are a-changing back.

David Pichaske **Bob Dylan Dreams of Home**

'Can't repeat the past?' he cried incredulously.
'Why of course you can!'

—Fitzgerald, *The Great Gatsby*

The eyes may stay forever young,
 and the rolling stone may tumble still,
 but feet walk through dead streets
 past foggy ruins of a fading past.

"Home" is an idea born in time.
The dream dries up when the sun goes down.
In a broken world, everything breaks.
Sign on the doorpost says "condemned."

The name on the mailbox is no longer yours.
A tattered curtain blows in the wind.
Just try going back to straighten things out:
You never get back all of the way.

Nobody knows who you're talkin' about,

and she's a big girl now. I doubt

she even remembers you at all.

"It's not dark yet, but it's gettin' there."

Catherine Pierce **Poem for Bob Dylan's Women**

How simple it must be, to be the woman in the song.

To know without doubt that you're magnetic

and precious, that you can shelter like God, that Honey,

you were Bob Dylan's true love and he's still weeping.

It must be some life, your mercury mouth full

of sighs that merit ballads, heat that feeds the blues.

But Sara, Louise, Sweet Melinda, Sweet Marie, let me ask you:

What is it like to wait in a room made of music?

Peggy Day, what happens when the song ends? Does he ever

come home? Maybe you hold out your hands to him,

hands like rivers, like doves, but Ruby, Queen Jane,

those are your words, not his. He didn't sing about your hands,

only your curls and your sadness. Maybe there's nothing

to touch him with at all. Maybe you reach out

with what you want to believe is beauty, but

he doesn't come to you, he stands in the doorway, sings

a song about a woman. You can see her next to him.

She is sad-eyed, long-haired. Her hands are just like yours.

Liza Porter **The Day My Brother Meets Bob Dylan**

The day my brother meets Bob Dylan, they're standing at a
crossroads in the heart of Iowa, yellow corn fields to the left and to
the right as far as the eye can see. The tour bus is broken
down halfway to the next town—Bob's playing all the state
fairgrounds this summer—and the dust rises up from the road like
a cloud of locusts during the Great Depression. They're wearing the same
thing—Bob Dylan and my brother—old jeans and white T-shirts and
worn out motorcycle boots, and my bro puts his hand out and says:
Honored to finally meet you, man. Bob bows down after the hand-
shaking and when he straightens up, he looks in front of him and
then behind and then to each side and then right into my
brother's eyes and says: This sure ain't no Highway 61, is it? And
my bro grins and after looking himself in all four directions, goes: no
it don't seem so, and then he lifts his eyes to the great song traveler's face and
says, you know, I can sing every word to every song you ever wrote, I
mean from the very beginning the very first song all the way up to now and
sometimes phrases come out of my mouth when I'm merely having a
conversation with someone, and I just want to tell you, man, I've wanted to
tell you this for years, man, I can't believe I finally have this chance, my
brother takes a big breath, and says: Thank you for giving me a voice.

And Bob just nods and goes: you're welcome, you're welcome, man, you
are only the second person to have the guts to say that to me, but you
know I can't take credit for it, I can't seem to help it the way these words come
pouring out of me, it started when I was still Zimmerman up in that freezing
cold Hibbing, Minnesota, and then someone threw a guitar into my hands, and
then later there was an old piano and that Hohner harmonica I got for
Hanukkah one year, that is my favorite thing, you know, the harmonica. And
everyone started clapping, before that it felt like a Zen thing, you know, that
one-ness that unity with the whole fucking planet with the music the words the
little blackbirds flying round my head speaking to me in tongues, but after the
clapping began, I was suddenly on this road that never ends on this tour that
never ends and I been on it ever since. And Bob looks around him, brushes some
dust off his pants with his right hand and looks at my bro again. You know, he
says, some people say I sold my soul to rock and roll and I say: so? Was there
ever any other choice? And they always drop their eyes and walk away, bummed
out, you see, because I don't have a reasonable explanation to tell them about
all that. And I'd like to know what you think. Bob's blue eyes are so intense my
bro thinks they'll bore into his brain and extract what exactly he is trying to
say, without him having to say it, and they stand there at the crossroads that
way for quite a while, the corn standing in quiet rows around them, the dust
flying, looking at each other, and my bro smiles his own blue-eyed smile and goes:

You know, Bob, can I call you Bob? and he waits for Bob to nod, and he says, I don't know anything about that thing you just said, about selling your soul to rock and roll, but I'm feeling a sort of déjà vu here, are you trying to say you sold your soul to the devil, like that blues man what was his name?—Robert Johnson?—like he did years ago, down in the Delta? Standing at that crossroads like we're doing here? You know, my bro says, I sold my soul to drugs and other horrible things long ago and am just now at the age of 55 buying it back. And if you think something like that happened to you, man, I am here to tell you, you can get it back, I am living proof you can get your soul back, I know you can, I know that. If I know anything at all, *I know that*. And he nods at Bob.

And then without thinking my bro starts quoting song lyrics up and down and sideways, the whole "lay down your weary tune" thing and "no one can sing the blues like Blind Willie McTell" and "God said to Abraham, give me a son," and "every grain of sand," and "ring them bells" especially every single word of "Masters of War", and "Sara" off the *Desire* record, and of course "Tangled Up in Blue" (the album version not the live one), and he says all of Bob's words as if he is reciting Walt Whitman reciting Allen Ginsberg reciting "Howl", or Rumi telling us what we need to know, my brother with his head bowed, he just can't help himself. And Bob stands there, hands in the pockets of his jeans, and listens with a serene look on his face, even though the wind is howling and the dust is

outrageous, rising almost to their shoulders by now, and with a flick of his
wrist, Bob takes his Hohner out of his back pocket and starts accompanying my
brother, who is singing now, not just reciting, and my bro's face turns upward to
the sky, he looks like a young choirboy now, and you can tell this is the very
best day of his entire life better even than the day he picked up drugs and
finally felt good, and better even than the day he put them down to save his life.

And Bob turns on his worn-down boot heel and starts walking west and my
bro turns too and follows him, and they both disappear into the swirling
brown dust and the golden cornfields and that idiot wind out in the middle of
nowhere, and who knows where they go next? You can bet it isn't in the
direction of no fairgrounds in the middle of nowhere, in the middle of Iowa,
no, no, no. I just don't think so.

Carol Kapaun Ratchenski **Sing Out Bob, Loud**

My friend saw him at the Purple Onion. My sister's husband was at Woodstock, amongst the betrayed and disillusioned, before Vietnam showed him what a broken promise really feels like. I saw him in a football stadium, a memory blurred by pot smoke and inaudible wisdom. Loud and mean and ungrateful truths in rhyme and meter. The predictable, stunning magic of four-four time. All that haze foretelling another purple magician who would romance us with boas and something to say both loud and mysteriously, soft and quiet. These two Minnesotans so unlike the rumored masses: straightforward, obvious, understated across generations of unvoiced screams. Injustice and sex and ecstasy, muffled on these northern plains, under down comforters and fields of barley, corn and sweet alfalfa. Here, lakeside or near the western valley, we live with the kind of winter that makes us all poets or crazy, often both. We need their ideals and their violence. We know our children will need to learn how to lose, how to grieve, how to let go, how to bury us young and how to love us anyway. So we argue and we judge. We pray for rain and settle for a generous raspberry crop. We crave forgiveness and we dance, in church basements and VFWs, in laundry rooms and in sunflower fields. When he turned sixty we couldn't believe it. When we knew he never would we couldn't believe it too.

John Reinhard **Bob Dylan Says**

When you're lost in the rain in Juarez

and it's Eastertime, too

makes no sense unless, perhaps,

it's April, you're in Mexico,

and Jesus Christ is rising a block

over. Now, I realize some people

think that listening to Bob Dylan sing is

like listening to fingernails keep time

against slate or to some blind monk chant

537 pages of *The Book of the Dead* or

to your favorite child

scrape the inner workings from a pet cat

in a sad attempt to shape

an organic violin, all twig and gut. But I'd argue

for Dylan as rain in drought; a girl

in her first uniform, smiling

with the authority of cloud;

a pencil, firmly pressed

on paper, no eraser.

Why not praise the voice

that is set in its ways and

spontaneous, both

at once. Actually, I was

like that, in another life, but

in Juarez with no language

except flowers, which were loud,

so I placed one in the hair of a woman

who was on her way to just around

the corner where Jesus H. Christ was

stretching his arms, singing, waking

the very dead.

Ellen Sander **Scuff**

Ever sit down and do it
just to see what would happen?

Let me give you some advice:
Don't try to do it while
Memphis Blues Again
is playing.

Judith Sanders **I Did Not Want to *Be* Bob Dylan**

although of course I worshipped him

as Shakespeare reincarnated

with nasal aspiration.

Why dream of being

a reclusive, verbally complex

revealer of hypocrisies,

a prophet only half understood,

when I already was one,

although not of the genius variety?

I wanted to be a man of the people like the Beatles

a rags-to-riches success like the Beatles

a magician of moods like the Beatles

always metamorphosing like the Beatles

without the familiar burden of intellectualism

and hyper-acute attunement to historical doom

salved by the glories of language

of judgment and prophecy,

of revelation and blessing,

mitigated by ironic inter-penetrations

of borrowed blues.

No, I did not care to be even more inscrutable.

I did not crave the solitary pulpit in the spotlight.

I'd rather be clowning with friends

in that empty field in *A Hard Day's Night*.

I didn't want to be the bard of break-ups,

an anatomizer of solitudes

already too familiar.

Not lonesome when you go,

not tangled in blue by a twist of fate,

but two of us, oh darlin', on our way home.

Patti Smith **dog dream**

have you seen

dylan's dog

it got wings

it can fly

if you speak

of it to him

it's the only

time dylan

can't look you in the eye

have you held

dylan's snake

it rattles like a toy

it sleeps in the grass

it coils in his hand

it hums and it strikes out

when dylan cries out

when dylan cries out

have you pressed

to your face

dylan's bird

dylan's bird

it lies on dylan's hip

trembles inside of him

it drops upon the ground

it rolls with dylan round

it's the only one

who comes

when dylan comes

have you seen

dylan's dog

it got wings

it can fly

when it lands

like a clown

he's the only

thing allowed

to look dylan in the eye

Gerard Smyth **A Jukebox in Minnesota**

A coin in a jukebox in Minnesota

was the price of a song

to placate the gods of St. Paul,

of Duluth where a greenhorn

heard the lovesick and rueful Opry star

and the bluesman, light-fingered

on his travelling guitar.

Highland snows were beginning to thaw

when out of that wilderness of iron ore

the singing man with harmonica

stepped into the arena, proclaimed a new order.

But it's no real life being the one

who has to stay *forever young*: a gypsy scholar

on speedway and ocean, and be as well

the shaman, messenger, joker

in tune with perpetual motion.

Father of Jacob, son of Abram, a Jack of Hearts

who like Lazarus received a second chance.

Timothy Steele **The Concert**

He soloed for the first half of the show,

A troubadour attempting to expand,

Then, following a short break, brought on stage

A band that would in time become The Band.

His folk fans left in protest and in droves.

Theirs was the music he had helped revive

And was, from their perspective, trashing now

In late October, nineteen sixty-five.

We young who stayed and listened were too quick

To pride ourselves on our enlightenment.

Substantial as he was, in years to come

We couldn't always follow where he went.

There were dismaying moments, from *Self Portrait*

To the bizarre Victoria's Secret ad;

During performances, he sometimes sounded

Willfully off-putting or downright bad.

"You saw him on his first electric tour?"
A friend said lately. "That must have been intense!"
It was. Yet, spot-lit, he looked thin and frail.
The night before, he'd played in Providence;
Detroit would be his next stop; and the mixed
Receptions he was getting wore on him.
After he closed with "Like a Rolling Stone,"
He vanished. The lights came on in the gym.

As we walked home in groups of two's and three's,
A creamy-haloed moon portended snow.
The wind swirled dry leaves at our feet, as if
Training to rope calves in a rodeo.
Somebody, having checked her watch, announced
Tonight had just turned into yesterday.
We hunched a little deeper in our coats
And went, with surer purpose, on our way.

J. J. Steinfeld **Perhaps the Answer is in a Flower Being Blown in the Wind**

...And I am dumb to tell the crooked rose

My youth is bent by the same wintry fever.

—Dylan Thomas, "The Force That Through the Green Fuse Drives the Flower"

In English class, near term's end,

the machinery of pedagogy chugging and clanking along,

your professor, a child of both the fifties and sixties,

on the verge of retirement,

or extinguishment,

as he drolly says, drawing on an unlit pipe,

speaks to his eager-to-leave class:

In the old days, before any of you took breath,

I puffed madly away as I lectured

even then I talked of the two big Ds

Dylan Thomas and Bob Dylan,

Dylan and Dylan,

sounds like a firm of creative accountants

itemizing images of our times.

Your professor laughs at his own words

a few in the class, like hired applauders, laugh along.

But today we deconstruct

I didn't deconstruct back then

I puffed contemplatively on my pipe

when pipe-smoking in this building wasn't *verboten*.

In class, you simultaneously deconstruct Bob Dylan's "Blowin' in the Wind"

and Dylan Thomas's "The Force That Through the Green Fuse Drives the Flower"

your professor lilting, I suggest that the answer is in a flower

being blown in the wind,

then asks: Is the flower on a city lawn or in a country meadow

or at the periphery of a garbage dump

or between the cracks of a sidewalk?

You, wanting to be a poet,

wanting to be somewhere else, ponder:

Is this cleverness or madness, your professor's words?

When I was a young professor, he lectures in a world-weary voice,

I sometimes brought a guitar to class

and sang my lecture, protest songs, an academic troubadour,

but I am now on the verge of extinguishment.

Maybe it is not too late, the professor says sadly to himself,

as if he had neglected to do something important earlier in the day,

but all in the class hear and no one weeps

as some had laughed before

though you think of weeping

as this man of erudition

regains composure, clears throat, bites on pipe stem,

continues like a death-defying orator:

Do you know that Dylan Thomas

died of a massive insult to the brain

also called alcohol poisoning

or drinking oneself to death?

Choose the unsympathetic description you prefer

yet Dylan Thomas is immortal

my definition of immortality at least

had he died peacefully in his sleep

about to taste eighty

would his immortality be less earned, less immortal?

I, myself, stopped drinking years ago,

but the pipe I cannot abandon,

a symbol of something enduring.

Our time is over

and we haven't even deconstructed

Bob Dylan's "The Times They Are A-Changin'"

or Dylan Thomas's "Love in the Asylum,"

which, incidentally, is my favourite poem.

Perhaps next class

my penultimate class

then my academic extinguishment

I will bring my old guitar.

You leave class

tossing thoughts of Dylan and Dylan to the sky and ground

and find a crooked flower

growing between the cracks

on a sidewalk close to your home

the flower, you decide,

the perfect replacement for the halls of academe.

The winter arrives secretively

burying the revelatory flower

you have been observing

you refusing to leave

contemplating your lost life

and the paths to immortality.

Heather Steinmann **Suspicious Male/
"Ballad of a Thin Man"**

He was more than drunk. Terrible dance with gravity to out-cold on my boulevard, shirtless, hair plastered to his head with the thick stain of wound. The dispatcher got the code all wrong: he wasn't suspicious, he was showing death his beautiful pirouette. The dispatch log should have read: So pale and so thin. So perfectly framed with bright green grass, long in need of cutting. The fireman pressed gauze to his head and his boy-like hand rose with the pain. He walked his fingers across that purple-gloved hand. Someone was touching his face. His surprise said that no one had done that in a long time. He touched someone back, and they stayed there. I wish I could tell him how the grass held the notion of his body, long after he was gone.

Marty Sternstein **Then Along Came Bob**

1) *That Time at the Supper Club*

He's covering a folk song that he's never sung in public:

    A willow has just bent and cried.

—Now he blinks into the klieg lights, rasps—

"Ah—

sh-

ucks!"

      His gleeful voice

demolishing the romantic dramas

that the words

suggest.

—Even the weeping willow grins.

2) *Bob and Van, Vaudevillians*

They've just dueted on a blues,

are patting each other on the back, smiling.

Then Dylan removes Morrison's hat,

points at his bald head,

and their smiles become laughter.

But "No Photographs Allowed"

—not that evidence of that kind

would have convinced anyone

that two described as "distant," "taciturn"

(and similar words and worse),

would have carried on so in public.

3) *Was He Possessed?*

That night at Tramps, when he sang "Visions of Johanna" *twice*—was he possessed?

Was he possessed in Connecticut some days earlier, when he wandered the stage
after the encores and while the arena was emptying,
pausing to look at each of the instruments as if he'd never seen them before,
while rubbing fiercely at his fierce hair?

My voodoo friend, her turbaned head on my shoulder, sighed, "Child, can you see, do you see?"
And me saying, "I wouldn't go that far."
And she insisting, "Look. See."

4) *Starbucks Plays Dylan*

Over the morning coffee hubbub, Dylan is singing "Buckets of Rain,"

a song that not too many people know.

The words *little red wagon* get drowned out by two laughing young women

who are still enjoying the night before—

"Did you?" "Do you remember?"

I've been there. I understand.

But Hush I want to say

—you may never get to hear these words again:

You do what you must do, and you do it well.

And now comes his young voice,

lost in the rain

in Juarez.

5) *1967*

Early in the year—
Sgt. Pepper! "Did you hear it! Did you hear!"
and *Satanic Majesties*, *Pillow*, Grace, "White Rabbit."
And all those jacket covers:
snip-and-paste portraits of friends and heroes and alter egos.

So we're waiting to hear what Bob will come up with, what kind of ultra surrealism,
something beyond "Johanna" and "Desolation Row,"
something that would have dumbfounded those French guys like Breton,
something beyond all manifestos.
We're waiting for the lid to blow.

And what does Bob do?
Along around Christmas comes an album with a cover that's a blown up snapshot
of him and three cronies who could be American Indians, though we're sure they're not.
And the songs are these simple story-songs, though of course they're not,
they're like ancient Scottish ballads like "Sir Patrick Spens"
in which significant events take place between verses.

And I say something about how professors will be lecturing on "Watchtower":
"Note the ending which is really a beginning," blah blah.

But my friend, schooled in Brechtian cunning, gets more to the point
—"It's Ju-jitsu, don't you see?

And Bob wins every time."

Joyce Sutphen **To Take Her Home**

Later, on the highway home, when she is

passing everything in sight, she looks

into the rearview mirror, expecting

a squad car, maybe, or a monster truck,

But there is nothing there, except the lights

of cars that are fading in the distance,

and now, there is nothing up ahead. Night

parts its dark waters down to the instant

When she is free—as wind, as speed, as this

song that she summons up again with just

the push of a button, and then the voice

riding the guitar and harmonica.

Whatever hard rain is going to fall

she knows—she's already heard it all.

Judy Swann **Live at the Beijing Workers' Gymnasium**

I explained it as well as I could, I said
Dylan is god and there is no god but Dylan,
a joke on Islam for the great Minnesotan.

Explain it to me better mother he said,
I said I don't wanna get side-tracked
right now, don't wanna preach to you

he said I can't make out the words cos
his voice is so scratchy and I said it's the trip
and was vaguely 3-D about the way

the light shone through his hair
on stage, the air thick with marijuana
but wait before that, on the way in

how I threw open my coat and shook
my chest at the bouncer so he could pat
me down for booze and recording equipment

who stopped and blinked his eyes once and said
"Waaaay too eager" and I and my ganja entered
believing in the power of love

and the knowledge of death, the ending up
little more than a mutt, not relationship material.
Tonight, pushing 70, in Shanghai

he wears a necklace of yaupon holly berries
and sings "My Wife's Home Town."

Russell Thorburn **Robbie Robertson
Sipping a Bitter Coffee
While Bob Dylan Types
His Next Song**

We are dying every day;

those clouds rose from her dark hair

when he was a boy and his Jewish father's

body was uncovered from the metal of a crash.

Next room, Dylan dances across

an old typewriter, and drums of the reservation

like Robbie's heartbeat ache

for everything to go away, his mother

a Mohawk who breathes through

his eyelids for him to hear those early songs

learned from the ghosts who walked

through the midnight drums.

Every morning he mops up sad-eyed

eggs he chased around the plate, and sees

his mother combing her long black hair,

as if every chord he'd ever play

had her fingers in it.

At Big Pink, the holes in the floor

leak the basement tapes trapped on reels,

the piano down there with its funny yellow teeth,

the drum set ready for radio—both

of them prophets, Robbie at the kitchen table,

a cigarette dangling from a lower lip,

as he hears Dylan slam back the carriage

as if still traveling in a Buick

with worn-out brakes and windows

rolled down for anything that goes by

on America's billboards fading into history.

Nothing left but grounds in his cup,

Robbie's fortune rides far and wide those Southern ruins

of his gothic muse, smoke pouring

from his mouth like cotton fields aflame.

Dylan strips the wrinkled page

from the platen and stands up, his cigarette

teeth-clenched, and shouts, "We are going

down in the flood," and Richard Manuel,

in his bear-like shadow, leans toward

the first step of the basement, behind Levon

in country short hair of a farmer

who's dreaming of his next crop.

But before Robbie sets down

his coffee cup, he looks outside at the crows

in their clothesline straight flight

into the huddled trees, Danko

striding out of them wearing his Billy

the Kid hat atop bushy hair,

as if he were coming straight from

a shootout, and again in his heartbeat,

restless sleep of a weight Robbie

can't ever lift, prays his mother to

forgive him for these guitar licks

and smoke that drifts without any words

like a religion he chords every day

in the biting steel strings of his Telecaster.

Chrys Tobey **Baby Blue**

You are paper,

thin between my fingers.

Soon you will rub apart.

You've become the words I hum—

It's all over now, Baby Blue...

The headlights are far away now

and before I can't see them anymore

I want to tell you something:

I was once happy with you.

I know, you're thinking I never

liked the word *happy.*

But the air smells

of dough here

and I'm beginning

to get used to the rain.

The people give me coffee

and the windows

are guitars that strum—

Forget the dead you've left,

they will not follow you.

Rodney Torreson **No Organ Player, Al Kooper Storms the Empty Hammond to Give a Song Its Signature Sound**

But first, from urban scurry he slips

into the studio as winds wail, filling his white shirt,

lapping his tie; he unsheathes his guitar like he

belongs. When the organist shifts to piano,

his bench becomes the new benchmark for empty.

Kooper, careless as always with uncertainty,

cons the moon and stars,

eases into that seat, as naturally as a yawn,

to show that he belongs.

It is rearranging tusks on an elephant

to feel he can own these ivories,

but that primal gnawing unearths the organ's sound

as Dylan behind sunglasses,

with truculence groans the wild brush:

"Once upon a time you dressed so fine /

threw the bums a dime, in your prime,"

the song dented up by drums,

then mixing it up just short of dust,

and Kooper, with fingers left over from the cave,

with the Hammond bone clubs the next meal,

the girl Dylan sings about with a hunger

that can't be shaken out in some discotheque,

stands in wilted shoes

as Dylan snarls and his voice writes lessons

in the dust, and Al Kooper feels

the pull of the earth, that eternal repertoire,

on keyboards writes the new hieroglyphics.

Katrina Vandenberg **Record**

Late night July, Minnesota,

John asleep on the glassed-in porch,

Bob Dylan quiet on cassette

you made from an album

I got rid of soon after

you died. Years later,

I regret giving up

your two boxes of vinyl,

which I loved. Surely

they were too awkward,

too easily broken

for people who loved music

the way we did. But tonight,

I'm in the mood for ghosts, for

sounds we hated: pop,

scratch, hiss, the occasional

skip. The curtains balloon;

I've got a beer; I'm struck

by guilt, watching you

from a place ten years away,

kneeling and cleaning each

with a velvet brush before

and after, tucking them in

their sleeves. Understand,

I was still moving then.

The boxes were heavy.

If I had known

I would stop here

with a husband to help me

carry, and room—too late,

the college kids pick over your

black bones on Mass. Ave., *we'll*

meet again some day

on the avenue but still,

I want to hear it,

the needle reaching the end

of a side and playing silence

until the arm gives up,

pulls away.

Anne Waldman **Excerpt from**

"Shaman Hisses You

Slide Back into the Night"

Dream: Dylan & «Don»

Allen Ginsberg & I go visit Dylan who's living in a series of cabins on a lake on the Lower East Side. He's seemingly in a dark mood for as we enter we find him attempting to climb into his guitar case like a coffin. Soothed by our sudden appearance he gestures toward some color Polaroid snapshots of his kids taken in the woods, which are balancing on the arm of a plush stuffed forest-green chair. We ask him about his work—his «book»—& he throws back a gruff laugh. As we go to let in more visitors including Clark Coolidge, Gregory Corso, and a girl desk clerk from the Hotel Boulderado, Dylan slips into one of the back cabins.

I take a walk in the woods and have a pearly white dagger handle thrown at me (which I catch) by a guy named «Don» who's standing on an embankment. He explains it is the «specialty of these woods.» Then he throws an entire dagger which stabs the ground at my feet & starts the whole place on fire.

Gregory & I have an interchange as the fire is ranging. He comments that my leather pants are «4 feet too long».

Everyone is frantic now trying to rescue books and papers & Bob himself who has locked himself into another one of the back cabins which is now in flames. I break the glass in the window & wake up.

mingle   calamity   moist   coda   gaping   adorns

tab   camaraderie   tantamount   gotta   leur   après

freeways   November   powder   patois   bust   weak

drenched   brass   loyal   Douglas   Connecticut   rain

lament   memorable   Phydeaux   Rome   Pasolini   unit

brandy   rock   Niagara   fatigue   indefatigable   prone

Roger   Gitane   seat   Ethan   Journal   shaman

wily   didatic   unshackle   away   deadlock   economy

Brazil   dream   dalliance   scores   chemistry   surly

diction   bleeding   clever   paint   red   multitudes

shadow   humble   river   shaman   yawns   holiday

obscure   tongue   die   ancient   children   horses

moving   tribe   gaping   decrees   urge   ally

river   further   navigating   shadow   imprinting   you

paragraphs   jaguar   chromium   timbrels   snaps   down

cleave   harbor   Chinese   modern   faun   wig

thousand   pains   shaman   ocean   obvious   centripetal

baby   guitar   gruff   compadre   American   meter

feather   brim   struts   kachina   hungry   clocks

Gitane   Rome   eyeballs   gesture   jive   sky

vocalize   vicissitudes   Danbury   coercion   bystander

gaping   kingdom   Egypt   Braille   Dot   meliorism

Byzantine   shaman   flickering   friction   moment   This a man-woman a shaman a man who makes a song to heal

a woman-man a sha-man a woman makes this song to heal

a mannerism a shaman has a man who plays a drum to heal

a woman signing a woman dancing a woman makes a place a meal

a spinning man a clay man a shaman takes your song for fuel

a watching woman-man a shaman watches & plans a song to make you well

a showman makes a song so smart to hear it swell

a woman-man a he-she man takes this place to steal the show

a man-woman a shaman woman makes the song appeal

steel man inside shaman gesture in blue

salmon color woman skin make her skin a drum to heal

1976

Connie Wanek **Two Degrees of Separation**

Twilight on the frozen lake

North wind about to break

On footprints in the snow

Silence down below

                              —Bob Dylan

Hannah's friend Chloe says

her parents have a couch

that once belonged to Bob Dylan.

Some years ago Lars was working downtown

and saw a guy who was almost certainly

Bob Dylan coming out of a shop

with an armload of t-shirts featuring Dylan

as drawn by Chris Monroe.

Who else would buy so many?

It was probably 1991 when the *News-Tribune*

published an article complaining

that Bob never mentioned Duluth in his songs,

and Phil wrote a letter to the editors

directing their attention to 1974's *Planet Waves*

wherein Dylan is "walkin' the hills of old Duluth,"

which he rhymes with "phantoms of my youth,"

and "truth," as well as "Ruth"

(and we all remember Ruth).

The letter was never published.

Sometime in the 80s our brother-in-law Scott

(to whom we haven't spoken in some time,

but that's another story) got a tip

that "someone special" was in town

visiting his friend Louis Kemp and staying

at a "certain Spirit Mountain condo."

So Scott parked his Johnson Controls van

right in front of the building for his

whole lunch hour.

But no one went in or out.

Down on the Lakewalk

we surreptitiously examine the oncoming faces,

especially the solitary, guarded ones

in the shadows of hat brims.

It's going to happen.

Michael Waters **The Captain's Tower**

I first heard the name Ezra Pound on Saturday, August 28, 1965, yawped by Bob Dylan in a new song, "Desolation Row," performed that night at Forest Hills Tennis Stadium in Queens, New York. I was fifteen.

And Ezra Pound and T.S. Eliot
Fighting in the captain's tower
While calypso singers laugh at them
And fishermen hold flowers
Between the windows of the sea
Where lovely mermaids flow
And nobody has to think too much
About Desolation Row

I had no idea that those three syllables formed a name. As they came near the beginning of the line, the syllables sounded more like "*every pound*"—"every pound of T.S Eliot." Such misheard lyrics constitute a *mondegreen*, the word coined by Sylvia Wright in an essay published in *Harper's Magazine* in 1954 and named after Lady Mondegreen. There was no Lady Mondegreen. The lines of an anonymous 17th century ballad, "They hae slain the Earl of Murray, / And laid him on the green," are misheard as "They hae slain the Earl of Murray and Lady Mondegreen." Popular song lyrics are rife with such misheard phrasings ("Hold me close and tie me down, sir"), but this time the fault was my own.

The album on which "Desolation Row" appeared, *Highway 61 Revisited*, would be released two days later, so during that week I spun the disc again and again and heard the name repeated until finally it came clear. It was obvious that Dylan had read "The Love Song of J. Alfred Prufrock":

> I have heard the mermaids singing, each to each.
> I do not think that they will sing to me.
> I have seen them riding seaward on the waves.

I had been reading Eliot. But Ezra Pound?

The following Saturday, on the final weekend of summer before high school resumed, I took the F train into lower Manhattan and walked off Sixth Avenue to the 8th Street Bookshop, "the very hearthside of hip, the cynosure of cool," *The New York Times* would claim three decades later. "[T]he person riffling through a book in the next aisle could be W. H. Auden... Marianne Moore... or perhaps Allen Ginsberg." The poetry books lined the upstairs wall to the right of the staircase, and you could cradle an armful to the front of that second floor where the literary journals wobbled in stacks and where one or two shabby easy chairs had been placed before the window above 8th Street: *the captain's tower*. That's where I slouched that afternoon with several books by Ezra Pound.

What did I read that day—"The River-Merchant's Wife: A Letter"? "In a Station of the Metro," its fourteen words leaping from ghostly human faces to "Petals on a wet, black bough"? "Hugh Selwyn Mauberley" with its "sudden shifts of perspective," its "presentation of an individual consciousness against a panorama of the age," as Richard Ellmann describes the poem? Didn't that also describe what Dylan was doing in "Desolation Row"? Pound was still alive in 1965. He suddenly seemed, as I sat in the 8th Street Bookshop, as vital a presence as The Beatles, as Dylan. "Ezra Pound," I mouthed to myself. Pop music was moving beyond me, and I had to be smarter to catch up.

David Wojahn **Woody Guthrie Visited by Bob Dylan:
Brooklyn State Hospital, New York, 1961**

He has lain here for a terrible, motionless

Decade, and talks through a system of winks

And facial twitches. The nurse props a cigarette

Between his lips, wipes his forehead. She thinks

He wants to send the kid away, but decides

To let him in—he's waited hours.

Guitar case, jean jacket. A corduroy cap slides

Down his forehead. Doesn't talk. He can't be more

Than twenty. He straps on the harmonica holder,

Tunes up, and begins his "Song to Woody,"

Trying to sound three times his age, sandpaper

Dustbowl growl, the song interminable, inept. Should he

Sing another? The eyes roll their half-hearted yes.

The nurse grits her teeth, stubs out the cigarette.

Anne Harding Woodworth **Flat Rock (NC) Visitor**

remembering a story about Robert Allen Zimmerman, February '64

At 22 he walks clumsily up the drive.
The bar at the Woodfield has closed,
and the boys have gone to bed.

But Bob's in search of poems, of songs—
hard to know in the early days
which way time and poetry will go.

His knock is loud.

The old poet opens the door and sniffs
at the young man's beery steam.
"I want to show you my poems," Bob says.

And this is where the story gets murky.
"Go your own way," the old man says.
"Poets cry only to themselves."

But in another version he says:

"I've been waiting for a knock on my door."

Either way, he leaves Bob alone on the glider.

Dozing, does Bob hear the door open again?

Does he see Carl Sandburg, framed by a light behind him,

scarf around his neck and holding two guitars?

Sandburg sits down next to Dylan, hands him an instrument.

They strum an E-major chord and begin to sing.

There's a wind. There's always a wind,

or is it just a ripple in the nearby hemlock

a few feet from the porch?

Baron Wormser **Dylanesque**

The river of plenty ran through my heart
Glimmered and glinted till you wrenched it apart.

I trusted your kiss, trusted your touch
Then you said love didn't amount to much,

Was a dog on the street, cloud in the sky,
A wish waiting for time to reply.

You could have been true though who knows when
A man and woman do more than pretend,

Form an angle that's less than oblique,
Or more than a mean blue streak

Through an inner prairie of glass.
I'm flat on my soul's lame ass

Holding a photo that's torn,
Chewing the scraps of your scorn.

We make stuff up then act like it's real.
That banquet, babe, was my last meal.

Charles Wright **When You're Lost in Juarez, in the Rain, and It's Easter Time Too**

Like a grain of sand added to time,

Like an inch of air added to space,

                                        or a half-inch,

We scribble our little sentences.

Some of them sound okay and some of them sound not so okay.

A grain and an inch, a grain and an inch and a half.

Sad word wands, desperate alphabet.

Still, there's been no alternative

Since language fell from the sky.

Though mystics have always said that communication is

        languageless.

And maybe they're right—

                                the soul speaks and the soul receives.

Small room for rebuttal there . . .

Over the Blue Ridge, late March late light annunciatory and

        visitational.

Tonight the comet Hale-Bopp

                                will ghost up on the dark page of the sky

By its secret juice and design from the full moon's heat.

Tonight some miracle will happen, it always does.

Good Friday's a hard rain that won't fall.

Wild onion and clump grass, green on green.

Our mouths are incapable, white violets cover the earth.

Lisa Zaran **August 17, 2005 ("Dear Bob Dylan")**

Dear Bob Dylan,

Pessoa says we never truly realize ourselves. We are like two chasms—a well staring up at the sky.

Arthur Rimbaud says it's as simple as a musical phrase.

Rainer Rilke says music: the breathing of statues. Perhaps: the silence of paintings. Language where language ends. Time that stands head-up in the direction of hearts that wear out.

I can't say anything. I can not speak, my tongue is broken. Sappho said that.

All my love,

Lisa

Liner Notes Thom Tammaro

Late autumn, 1965. 7:30 AM. I'm in my bedroom sitting on the edge of my bed, reading the liner notes to *Highway 61 Revisited*, "On the slow train time does not interfere..." and listening to "Just Like Tom Thumb's Blues" and "Desolation Row" repeatedly on Side 2. I have to lift the tone arm of my RCA Hi-Fi each time and set it in the right groove to repeat the two-song sequence totaling sixteen minutes and fifty-three seconds. I'm on the cusp of fourteen, and in ninth grade. My mother is yelling for me to get moving or I'll be late for school. Repeat. Repeat. Repeat. The ten-block walk to school in damp, drizzly western Pennsylvania November. Steel mill fires flaring in the dawn light. Yes, I am late for school.

Listening to those two songs becomes part of my early morning ritual for weeks. The lyrics burn themselves inside my head. I don't know yet that Dylan is channeling Rimbaud's "My Bohemian Life." Or that the writing style and technique have names—surrealism and stream-of-consciousness. (Dylan is writing *Tarantula* around this time, but it wouldn't be published until 1971). Given the nightmarish visions in both of those songs, you might think I was on the verge of leaping off childhood's precipice into the void of adolescent angst. But I don't remember myself as an angsty teen.

Rather, I went off to school those autumn mornings mesmerized by language. And it was there, about this time, and with the good fortune of having a couple of fine English teachers, that I began to discover metaphor and simile, narrative and allegory, image and sound. The dance of syllables across the page. I'm about to learn that language is symbolic. Convergences that would alter my life forever. To borrow from a Neruda poem: "And it was at that age ... Poetry arrived in search of me"

("Poetry"). I came to poetry (and literature) because of Dylan. I came to Dylan because of his language—or I should say that Dylan came to me through his language. Foremost for me, listening to Dylan has always been a literary experience: "Don't Think Twice, It's All Right." "Visions of Johanna." "Positively 4th Street." "Sad Eyed Lady of the Lowlands." "Just Like a Woman." "All Along the Watchtower." "Tomorrow is a Long Time." "Forever Young."

Of course, that language was delivered in music. Is there a more perfect song than "Don't Think Twice, It's All Right?" Sometimes narratives sans choruses. But for me, as it was then, sitting on the edge of my bed reading Dylan's liner notes, it always has been about the language. Years later, I read an interview with Joni Mitchell in *Rolling Stone*. She remarked, "And when I heard 'Positively 4th Street' [1964], I realized that this was a whole new ballgame; now you could make your songs literature. The potential for the song had never occurred to me."

And so these one hundred poems—conversations, communions, improvisations, colloquies, riffs, meditations, parleys, dialogues, arguments with Dylan's life and work. On the slow train, time does not interfere.

Liner Notes Alan Davis

I was born a few minutes after midnight in New Orleans on June 30, 1950, the exact midpoint of the twentieth century. I came out of my mother butt first, a breech birth pulled out with forceps, my introduction to technology, and I've been trying to turn time around ever since. Up in Minnesota—Hibbing, to be exact, not so far (as the crow flies) from where I live now—Bob Dylan (born Robert Allen Zimmerman) was nine. I grew up near the mouth of the Mississippi and he was close to its headwaters. That makes us almost kin.

Since then, though I've attended a number of his concerts, we've met only once, in the French Quarter in 1976. I was a counselor for the Louisiana Department of Corrections. He was in town with his Rolling Thunder Revue to play a concert at The Warehouse in New Orleans. He was very slender of build when he stood next to me, introducing himself as "Frank," on the corner of Bourbon and St. Peter Streets, and asked for a smoke. I'm only five foot ten or so, but I was a few inches taller than he was, and it surprised me, because he had been a larger-than-life hero of mine ever since I had heard his surreal, city music in the late sixties—songs like "Ballad of a Thin Man" and "Stuck Inside of Mobile"—on 50,000 watt late night radio.

I gave him a smoke and a light. His song "Hurricane" had just been released. "Hey," I said, "will you come out to Jackson Barracks on the edge of town and play a set for the prisoners I work with?" He had on a cheap Musketeer hat with a red feather in it. "Prisoners?" he said. He was high on something. He smirked, touched the brim of his hat, and turned, as if on a dime, to disappear into a daiquiri bar where a bouncer the size of a boar kept out those of us without a ticket.

After Thom and I started working on this anthology, Dylan received the Nobel Prize in Literature, which I celebrated, though some were puzzled and even distraught, and I remembered that moment between us, just me and Bob, which I had dramatized in my story "Bringing It All Back Home" (available in *So Bravely Vegetative*). Dylan is famously difficult to pin down. That's exactly as it should be. In August of 2017, I paid a visit to the Nobel Museum in Stockholm. My tour guide there told me, when we talked after the tour, that Pearl Buck, not Dylan, is the one they regret. "We now have the Pearl Buck rule," he said. "We never pick a laureate the first few times they're nominated."

Does Dylan deserve such literary beatification? The prolific writer Baron Wormser, whose new, audacious novel *Tom O' Vietnam* is available from New Rivers Press, when asked who influenced him, said "... if you're willing to allow that a lyricist is a poet then Bob Dylan has been a Shakespeare to me. It's a rare day when some Dylan lines aren't in my head" (cavankerrypress.org). I couldn't agree more. The bounty of poems in this anthology bear undeniable witness to his influence and his vision. He contains multitudes. Thank you, Bob, for keeping time in mind all these years. I look forward to our next meeting.

Bio Note Chris Smither

Chris Smither—singer, songwriter, guitarist, essayist, short story writer, film scorer—grew up in New Orleans where he first started playing music as a child, heavily influenced by the blues, especially the music of Lightnin' Hopkins. At the urging of legendary folk singer Eric von Schmidt, Smither left college and headed to Boston, where he forged lifelong friendships with many musicians, including Bonnie Raitt who went on to record his songs, "Love You Like A Man" and "I Feel the Same." Smither has recorded more than twenty albums, including live recordings and compilations. For the past five decades, Smither has toured nationally and internationally to great reception and acclaim, cementing his reputation as one of the finest acoustic musicians in the country.

His album, *Small Revelations* (1997), climbed the Americana and Triple A radio charts and led to concert dates with B. B. King, Bonnie Raitt, Nanci Griffith, and the hugely successful, original Monsters of Folk tour with Ramblin' Jack Elliott, Dave Alvin, and Tom Russell. *Small Revelations* also generated several film projects for Smither. Emmylou Harris recorded his song, "Slow Surprise," for the *The Horse Whisperer* soundtrack. To *Train Home* (2003), Bonnie Raitt graciously provided backing vocals and slide guitar on Smither's haunting cover of Bob Dylan's "Desolation Row."

In 2005, jazz great Diana Krall covered Chris's "Love Me Like A Man," introducing what is now a blues standard to a whole world of jazz fans. To his 12th album, *Leave the Light On* (2006), Smither invited good friend and Grammy Award-winning multi-instrumentalist Tim O'Brien, along with rising American roots stars Ollabelle, to add their distinctive talents on several tracks. *Leave the Light On* also includes Chris's beautiful cover of Dylan's "Visions of Johanna."

Chris Smither Lyrics 1966–2012, with introductory commentary by poet Lisa Olstein and photographs from Chris' life side by side with his lyrics, is a complete collection of all of Chris' lyrics to date. In March 2018, Smither's eighteenth album, *Call Me Lucky*, debuted #2 on the Billboard Blues Chart.

https://smither.com

CONTRIBUTORS

HAL ACKERMAN lives in Brooklyn, NY. His play *Testosterone: How Prostate Cancer Made A Man of Me* was the recipient of the William Saroyan Centennial Prize for drama. Under its new title, *Prick*, it won Best Script at the 2011 United Solo Festival. "Belle & Melinda" was selected by Robert Olen Butler as the "World's Best Short Short" for *Southeast Review*.

LIZ AHL is the author of *Beating the Bounds* (2017), and three chapbooks of poetry, most recently, *Talking About the Weather* (2012). She has been awarded residencies at Jentel, Playa, The Kimmel Harding Nelson Center for the Arts, and The Vermont Studio Center. She lives in Holderness, New Hampshire.

ROBERT ALEXANDER has published two books of prose shorts—*White Pine Sucker River* (1993), and *What the Raven Said* (2006)—and a narrative history of the Civil War—*Five Forks: Waterloo of the Confederacy* (2003). His most recent book is *The Northwest Ordinance: Constitutional Politics and the Theft of Indian Land* (2017). He is the founding editor of the Marie Alexander Poetry Series at White Pine Press. He lives in Madison, WI.

JOEL ALLEGRETTI is the author of five collections of poetry, most recently *The Body in Equipoise* (2015), a chapbook on the theme of architecture and design. His second book, *Father Silicon* (2006), was selected by *The Kansas City Star* as one of 100 Noteworthy Books of 2006. He is the editor of *Rabbit Ears: TV Poems* (2015), the first anthology of poetry about the mass medium. He lives in Fort Lee, New Jersey.

DEVON BALWIT teaches in Portland, OR. She is the author of six chapbooks, among them *How the Blessed Travel* (2017), *Forms Most Marvelous* (2017), and *In Front of the Elements* (2017). Bob Dylan inspired her to write poetry, think outside the box, and not be afraid to change allegiance and identity as many times as it took.

ALIKI BARNSTONE is a poet, translator, critic, editor, and visual artist. She is the author of eight books of poetry, most recently, *Dwelling* (2016). Her translation, *The Collected Poems of C. P. Cavafy*, was published in 2006. She is Professor of English and Creative Writing at the University of Missouri and serves as poet laureate of Missouri. Bob Dylan has been part of the soundtrack of her life ever since she was a girl.

MARGE BARRETT has published a poetry chapbook, *My Memoir Dress*; stories in Dzanc Books' *Best of the Web 2009;* the Minnesota Historical Society's, *The State We're In*; and poetry and prose in numerous journals. She teaches at the Loft Literary Center in Minneapolis and conducts a variety of workshops.

ANNE BECKER, poet and teacher, lives in Takoma Park, MD. Her most recent collection of poems is *Human Animal* (2018). She began writing poems as a teenager, in the mid-'60s. Her muses were T.S. Eliot, Dylan Thomas, and Bob Dylan. As time passed, she felt that Bob Dylan had been one of America's best poets in those few years in the 60s. She continued to listen to his work up to his Christian phase and then dropped out. Given a cassette of *Under a Red Sky*, she was horrified—

galvanized into action. She sent him a postcard: "What I regret, what I miss is the relationship you used to have with words. Pick it up again—it's yours." Not receiving a reply, she wrote "Lament for Bob Dylan."

MADELEINE BECKMAN is the author of three collections of poems: *Hyacinths from the Wreckage* (2015); *No Roadmap, No Brakes* (2015); and *Dead Boyfriends*, first published by Linear Arts Books and reissued by Limoges Press (2012). She is a Contributing Reviewer to the *Bellevue Literary Review* and a Contributing Editor with *Agora: Literature and Arts Journal* (NYU Medical School). She is an Instructor with NYU School of Medicine, in the Medicine & Humanism Program.

MARVIN BELL's recent books include *After the Fact: Scripts & Postscripts* (2016), a dialogue in paragraphs of poetic nonfiction with Christopher Merrill, and *Vertigo: The Living Dead Man Poems* (2011). He lives in Iowa City, Iowa, and Port Townsend, Washington. Retired from the Iowa Writers' Workshop, he teaches for the brief-residency MFA located in Oregon at Pacific University. Bell's songwriter son, Nathan, has said, "Before Bob Dylan, nobody would allow a songwriter the space to think of himself as a serious writer."

TARA BETTS is the author of *Break the Habit* and *Arc & Hue* as well as the chapbooks *7x7: kwansabas* and *THE GREATEST!: An Homage to Muhammad Ali*. Tara holds a Ph.D. from Binghamton University and a MFA from New England College. She currently teaches at the University of Illinois-Chicago.

ROBERT BLY's numerous collections of translations, anthologies, criticism, and poetry make him one of the most influential poets of his generation. Bly won the 1968 National Book Award for poetry for his book, *The Light Around the Body* (1967). His latest collections of poems are: *Stealing Sugar from the Castle: Selected and New Poems, 1950 to 2013* (2016), *Like the New Moon I Will Live My Life* (2015), and *Talking into the Ear of a Donkey* (2011). *Airmail: The Letters of Robert Bly and Tomas Tranströmer* was published in 2013. *More Than True: The Wisdom of Fairy Tales* (2018), continues his nonfiction exploration of fairy tales, myth, and human nature begun with his best-selling *Iron John* (1990). He lives in Minneapolis, MN. His *Collected Poems* will be published in October 2018

JOHN BRADLEY is the author of eight books of poetry and prose, the most recent *Erotica Atomica* (2017). Like Bob Dylan, Bradley attended the University of Minnesota. He still can see that photo of young Bob at the typewriter, which was published in the *Minnesota Daily* as a recruitment ad for student journalists.

MICHAEL BROCKLEY is a retired school psychologist who worked in rural northeast Indiana. Recent poems have appeared in *Flying Island*, *Zingara Poetry Picks*, *Panoplyzine*, *Third Wednesday*, *The Gyroscope Review*, *Atticus Review*, *3Elements Review*, and *Gargoyle*. He lives in Muncie, Indiana.

NICOLE BROOKS is a writer and dance teacher living in Lafayette, Indiana. She holds degrees in dance and creative writing, and a master's in journalism. Nicole reported daily news and feature stories for newspapers in Indiana and Illinois, and worked as a reporter and producer for National

Public Radio in Bloomington, Indiana. Currently she is an associate director of marketing at Purdue University and is involved with the Lafayette Writers' Studio.

CHARLES BUKOWSKI, beloved by European readers, and one of America's best-known contemporary writers of poetry and prose, was born in 1920 in Andernach, Germany, to an American soldier father and a German mother, and brought to the United States at the age of two. He was raised in Los Angeles and lived there for more than fifty years. He published more than sixty collections of poems and prose during his lifetime, among them: *Post Office* (1971), *Mockingbird Wish Me Luck* (1972), *Factotum* (1975), *Love is a Dog from Hell* (1977), *Ham on Rye* (1982), and *War All the Time: Poems 1981–1984* (1984). More than thirty-five posthumous collections of poems, letters, notes, and prose have been published since his death in 1994, most recently, *Storm for the Living and the Dead: Uncollected and Unpublished Poems* (2017). *Born into This*, a documentary film on Bukowski, was released in 2003.

SIDNEY BURRIS lives in Fayetteville, Arkansas. He is the author of *Doing Lucretius: Poems* (2000) and *A Day at the Races* (1989). He teaches at the University of Arkansas, where he has directed the Fulbright College Honors Program for more than twenty-three years. A Seamus Heaney scholar, Burris is the author of *The Poetry of Resistance: Seamus Heaney and the Pastoral Tradition* (1990). He also directs The TEXT Program, an oral history project dedicated to recording the stories of Tibetan refugees living in exile.

EDWARD BYRNE is the author of eight collections of poetry and the editor of two anthologies. His works also have appeared in numerous literary journals—including *American Literary Review, American Poetry Review, American Scholar, Missouri Review, North American Review, Quarterly West*, and *Southern Humanities Review*—as well as an assortment of anthologies. Byrne is a professor of American literature and creative writing at Valparaiso University, where he serves as the editor of *Valparaiso Poetry Review.*

DAVID CAPPELLA, Professor Emeritus of English and 2017/2018 Poet-in-Residence at Central Connecticut State University, has co-authored two widely used poetry textbooks, *Teaching the Art of Poetry: The Moves* and *A Surge of Language: Teaching Poetry Day to Day.* His chapbook, *Gobbo: A Solitaire's Opera*, won the Bright Hill Press Poetry Chapbook Competition in 2006. He recently published a novel, *Kindling* (2016).

DAMIAN A. CARPENTER received a Ph.D. from Texas A&M University in 2014 and is currently a post-doctoral fellow at East Tennessee State University. He specializes in Outlaw Studies, Southern Literature, folk music and culture, and creative writing. *Lead Belly, Woody Guthrie, Bob Dylan and American Folk Outlaw Performance* (2017), examines the rhetoric and performance of the American folk outlaw.

JOHNNY CASH, singer, songwriter, musician, author, and actor, is an American cultural icon. During his half-century career, Cash recorded more than fifty-five studio albums and over one-hundred compilation albums, soundtracks, and collaborations. His Grammy-winning liner notes, "Of Bob Dylan," appeared on the back cover of Dylan's 1969 album, *Nashville Skyline*. Upon Cash's passing in 2003, Dylan wrote, "In plain terms, Johnny was and is the North Star; you could guide your ship by him—the greatest of the greats then and now."

JAN CHRONISTER lives and writes in the woods near Maple, Wisconsin. She has read poems at the annual Duluth Dylan Fest. A retired English instructor, Jan continues to teach poetry writing classes through Lake Superior Writers and adult education. Her work appears in many publications including *Sky Island Journal, The Wild Word, Plath Poetry Project* and *Pure Slush* as well as anthologies from, among others, Zoetic Press and Truth Serum Press. A full-length collection of her poetry is scheduled for publication in fall 2018.

ROCCO DE GIACOMO is the author of three collections of poetry: *Brace Yourselves* (2018), *Every Night of Our Lives* (2016), and *Ten Thousand Miles Between Us* (2009). His chapbook, *Catching Dawn's Breath*, was published in 2008. He lives in Toronto with his wife, Lisa Keophilia, a fabric artist, and his two daughters.

THEODORE DEPPE was born in Duluth, MN. He is the author of four collections of poetry, most recently *Beautiful Wheel* (2014) and *Orpheus on the Red Line* (2009), and his poems have appeared in many literary journals and magazines including *Harper's Magazine, The Kenyon Review, Poetry, Ploughshares, Poetry Ireland* Review, and *The Southern Review*. He directs the Stonecoast MFA in

Ireland program. He worked previously as a nurse for more than two decades in coronary care units and psychiatric hospitals. He lives in Connemara, Ireland.

DIANE DI PRIMA, artist, memoirist, playwright, and social activist, is the author of more than fifty books, among them: *The Poetry Deal* (2014), *Pieces of a Song: Selected Poems* (1990), *Recollections of My Life as a Woman: The New York Years* (2001), and the classic *Memoirs of a Beatnik* (1969; rpt. 1988). You can see and hear her read "Revolutionary Letter #4" in *The Last Waltz*, Martin Scorsese's magnificent film of The Band's farewell concert. Her collection *Revolutionary Letters* (1971) is dedicated to Bob Dylan.

THEO DORGAN is an Irish poet, novelist, prose writer, editor, essayist, and translator. Among his recent publications are: *Liberty Walks Naked* (2015), translations from the French of the Syrian poet Maram al-Masri; *Jason and the Argonauts* (2014), a libretto; *Foundation Stone: Towards a Constitution for A 21st Century Republic* (2013, editor) and the novel *Making Way* (2013). He was the 2010 winner of The O'Shaugnessy Award for Irish Poetry (USA). His most recent collection of poems, *Nine Bright Shiners,* was awarded the Irish Times/Poetry Now Prize for best collection published in 2014. A new collection, *Orpheus*, is forthcoming in early 2018. He is a member of Aosdána, Ireland's Academy of The Arts.

STEPHEN DUNN is the author of sixteen collections of poems, among them: *Whereas: Poems (2017), Lines of Defense (2013), Here and Now (2011), and What Goes On: Selected and New Poems*

(2009). Different Hours (2002) won the 2001 Pulitzer Prize for Poetry. His prose is collected in *Walking Light: Memoirs and Essays on Poetry (2001),* and *Riffs and Reciprocities: Prose Pairs (1998)*. He is Distinguished Professor Emeritus of Creative Writing at Stockton University in New Jersey. He lives in Frostburg, Maryland.

SUSAN ELBE is the author of *The Map of What Happened* (2013), winner of the 2012 Backwaters Press Prize and the Jacar Press 2014 Julie Suk Prize for the best book of poetry published by an independent press in 2013; *Eden in the Rearview Mirror* (2007); *Where Good Swimmers Drown* (2012), winner of the 2011 Concrete Wolf Chapbook Prize; and *Light Made from Nothing* (2003). She lives in Madison, WI.

LAWRENCE FERLINGHETTI co-founded City Lights, the first paperback bookstore in the United States. His *A Coney Island of the Mind* is iconic in contemporary literature, having sold more than one million copies since its publication in 1958. Author of more than fifty collections of poetry, prose, and letters, Ferlinghetti continues to paint and write as he approaches his 100th birthday. *Ferlinghetti's Greatest Poems* was published in 2017. Bob Dylan has called him "A brave man and a brave poet."

JEFF FRIEDMAN is the author of six collections of poetry, most recently *Floating Tales* (2017). His poems, mini-stories, and translations have appeared in many literary magazines, including *American Poetry Review, New England Review, North American Review, Poetry International,* and *The New*

Republic. With Dzvinia Orlowsky, he was awarded a National Endowment of the Arts Literature Translation Fellowship for their translations of poems by the Polish poet and translator Mieczyslaw Jastrun, resulting in the publication, *Memorials: A Selection* (2014). Friedman lives in West Lebanon, New Hampshire, and teaches at Keene State College.

DAVID GAINES is the author of *In Dylan Town: A Fan's Life* (2015), a book about his life as a Dylan fan and teacher at Southwestern University in Georgetown, Texas. He has been listening to and sharing Dylan since the mid-1960s and is proud to say that his four children can hold their own in Dylan circles.

CECILIA GIGLIOTTI is studying for the MA in English literature at Central Connecticut State University, though you may often find her in New York City, most recently tracing Dylan's early steps through Greenwich Village. Her current research examines Jack Kerouac's influence on Dylan's lyrical style. Publications include the personal essay "The Open Road" in the online literary magazine *Outrageous Fortune*, and the poem "Meditation on a Midnight Mass" in Susquehanna University's *RiverCraft*.

ALLEN GINSBERG was born in Newark, New Jersey, in 1926. After graduating from Paterson's East Side High School in 1943, Ginsberg attended Columbia College in New York, where he met William S. Burroughs, Neal Cassady, and Jack Kerouac. Ginsberg first met Dylan in 1963 and recorded with him in October-November 1971, in 1976, and in 1982. He also toured with Dylan in 1975-76 as a member of Dylan's Rolling Thunder Review and appeared in *Renaldo and Clara*. Among Ginsberg's numerous collections of poetry are: *Kaddish and Other Poems* (1961); *Reality Sandwiches* (1963); *The Fall of America: Poems of These States, 1965-1971* (1973), winner of the National Book Award; and *Mind Breaths: Poems 1971-1976* (1976). *Collected Poems 1947-1997* was published in 2006. With Ann Waldman, he co-founded and directed the Jack Kerouac School of Disembodied Poetics at the Naropa University in Colorado, and later he became a Distinguished Professor at Brooklyn College. He died in 1997.

BENJAMIN GOLUBOFF, fan more of Ginsberg than Dylan, is Associate Professor of English at Lake Forest College. In addition to some scholarly publications, he has placed imaginative writing in many small press journals over the years. Goluboff is the author of *Ho Chi Minh: A Speculative Life in Verse and Other Poems* (2017).

RAY GONZALEZ teaches creative writing and literature at the University of Minnesota. He is the author of fifteen books of poetry, including *Beautiful Wall* (2015), *The Hawk Temple at Tierra Grande* (2002), and *Turtle Pictures* (2001), all Minnesota Book Award winners. He is the author of three essay and two short story collections, as well as the editor of twelve anthologies, most recently *Sudden Fiction Latino: Short-Short Stories from the United States and Latin America* (2010). He was selected for the 2017 Witter Bynner Fellowship by the 21st Poet Laureate at the Library of Congress, Juan Felipe Herrera. Without Bob Dylan, he says, he could never write poetry.

JULIANA GRAY is the author of three poetry collections, *Honeymoon Palsy* (2017), *Roleplay* (2013), and *The Man Under My Skin* (2005). Her poems have appeared in *Best American Poetry, American*

Life in Poetry, and numerous journals. When she was a baby, every Sunday morning, her father would play "Sweet Jane Approximately," thereby indoctrinating a young Dylan fan. An Alabama native, Gray is a professor of English at Alfred University in western New York.

GEORGE GREEN's book, *Lord Byron's Foot* (2012), won the *New Criterion* Poetry Prize, the Poet's Prize, and an Academy Award from the American Academy of Arts and Letters. *Visiting Bob* is the ninth anthology in which his poetry has appeared. He lives in Manhattan and is an adjunct English Professor at Lehman College. A huge "pre-motorcycle-accident fan," Green became radically disenchanted by *Self Portrait* and the later recordings.

JEFF GUNDY's seven books of poems include *Abandoned Homeland* (2015) and *Somewhere Near Defiance* (2014). His most recent prose book is *Songs from an Empty Cage: Poetry, Mystery, Anabaptism, and Peace* (2013). He teaches writing and literature at Bluffton University in Ohio, and has spent sabbaticals as a Fulbright lecturer in Salzburg and, most recently, at LCC International University in Klaipeda, Lithuania. In the late sixties he somehow procured a copy of Dylan's early *Greatest Hits*. When his father heard the sounds emerging from the family's large console record player, he said, "That guy isn't bad on the harmonica, but do you really think he can sing?"

MARGARET HASSE, originally from South Dakota, now lives in Saint Paul, Minnesota, where she writes, teaches poetry workshops, and is involved with other literary projects. In 1973, soon after she moved to Minnesota, she bought a guitar in order to strum some of Dylan's songs. Recent collections of poems include, *Stars Above, Stars Below,* reissued in 2018, and *Between Us* (2016), winner of the 2016 Midwest Book Award in poetry.

MICHAEL HETTICH has published over a dozen books and chapbooks of poetry, including *The Frozen Harbor* (2017), recipient of the David Martinson-Meadowlark Prize; *Systems of Vanishing* (2014), recipient of the Tampa Prize for Poetry; *The Measured Breathing* (2011), winner of the Swan Scythe Press Award; and *Flock and Shadow: New and Selected Poems* (2005), a national Book Sense Spring 2006 Top Ten Poetry Book. He has listened seriously to Dylan since about 1965 when, driving to a Yankees game with his parents, "Blowin' in the Wind" came on the radio to blow him away. That voice has been singing in his head ever since.

TONY HOAGLAND is the author of six collections of poetry, most recently, *Priest Turned Therapist Treats Fear of God: Poems (2018); Application for Release from the Dream (2015); and Unincorporated Persons in the Late Honda Dynasty (2010).* He is also the author of two collections of essays about poetry, *Twenty Poems That Could Save America (2014)* and *Real Sofistakashun* (2006). His poems and critical essays have appeared widely in journals and anthologies such as *American Poetry Review, Harvard Review,* and *Ploughshares.* Hoagland currently teaches in the poetry program at the University of Houston.

HOLLY IGLESIAS has published two collections of poetry—*Angles of Approach* (2010) and *Souvenirs of a Shrunken World* (2008)—and one work of literary criticism, *Boxing Inside the Box:*

Women's Prose Poetry (2004). In addition, she has translated the work of Cuban poets Caridad Atencio and Nicolás Padrón. She has received fellowships from the National Endowment for the Arts, the North Carolina Arts Council, the Edward Albee Foundation, and the Massachusetts Cultural Council. Iglesias currently teaches in the MFA Program in Creative Writing at the University of Miami.

LOWELL JAEGER, as editor of Many Voices Press, compiled *New Poets of the American West*, an anthology of poets from eleven Western states. He is author of six collections of poems, including *How Quickly What's Passing Goes Past* (2013) and *Driving the Back Road Home* (2015). Most recently Jaeger was awarded the Montana Governor's Humanities Award for his work in promoting thoughtful civic discourse.

DIANE JARVENPA, singer, songwriter, guitarist, and kantele player (Finnish folk harp), is a versatile performer of folk and world music. Her collections of poems include *The Way She Told Her Story* (2017); *swift, bright, drift* (2016); *The Tender, Wild Things* (2007); and *Divining the Landscape* (1996). As Diane Jarvi, her CD recordings, *Foreign Winds*, *Revontuli*, *Flying Into Blue*, *Paper Heart*, *Wild Gardens* and *Bittersweet*, are heard on radio throughout Europe, Australia, Canada as well as · around the U.S. She is known in Finland as the Minnesotan Satakieli—The Minnesota Nightingale.

MELISSA FITE JOHNSON lives with her husband in Kansas, where she teaches English at her old high school. Her first collection, *While the Kettle's On* (2015), is a Kansas Notable Book, and her chapbook, *A Crooked Door Cut into the Sky* (2018), won the 2017 Vella Chapbook Award. When she was sixteen, Bob Dylan's "Blowin' in the Wind" played at her father's funeral.

ANDREW JONES is the author of a chapbook, *Moving Like Dim Ghosts* (2016). He lives near the Mississippi River on the edge of Iowa and teaches writing at the University of Dubuque.

NALINI JONES is the author of a story collection, *What You Call Winter* (2007). Her fiction has appeared in *One Story, Elle India,* and *Ontario Review*, and her essays in *Freud's Blind Spot* (2010) and *AIDS Sutra* (2008), among other publications. Her story, "Tiger," was the recipient of a 2013 Pushcart Prize, and in 2012 she received a Literature Fellowship from the National Endowment for the Arts. Jones lives in Connecticut and teaches at Columbia University's School of the Arts. She has worked as an associate producer or backstage manager for music festivals in Newport and New Orleans.

GEORGE KALAMARAS, former Poet Laureate of Indiana (2014-2016), is the author of fifteen books of poetry, eight of which are full-length, including *Kingdom of Throat-Stuck Luck*, winner of the Elixir Press Poetry Prize (2011). He is Professor of English at Indiana University-Purdue University Fort Wayne, where he has taught since 1990. He writes, "I've heard Dylan everywhere—from growing up with his songs, to his legacy in contemporary music, to Indiana rain through the leaves of sycamore trees."

SUSAN DOBLE KALUZA lives and works in Butte, Montana. Her poems have been published or are forthcoming in *Kentucky Review*, *Rattle*, and *Eunoia Review*. She recalls writing her Dylan poem a few years ago when she was reminiscing about her college days, studying under a dim book light while her roommate slept, and Dylan's voice crooned "Sara" from a cassette deck.

GERHARD KOFLER was an Austrian/Italian poet who lived in Vienna, wrote in Italian and German. "Bob Dylan in Detroit" is from *Poesie di mare, terra e cielo / Poesie von Meer, Erde und Himmel* (*Poetry of Sea, Earth and Sky*, 2003). Kofler and translator Geoff Howes, both longtime fans, saw Dylan for the first time in Detroit on Nov. 9, 2001.

YUSEF KOMUNYAKAA is the author of sixteen collections of poetry, including *The Emperor of Water Clocks* (2016), *Pleasure Dome: New and Collected Poems* (2004), and *Neon Vernacular New & Selected Poems 1977-1989* (1993), winner of the 1994 Pulitzer Prize for Poetry. *Condition Red: Essays, Interviews, Commentaries* was published in 2017. In 1999, he was elected a Chancellor of the Academy of American Poets. He is a senior faculty member in New York University's Creative Writing Program.

NORBERT KRAPF is the author of eleven collections of poems, most recently, *Catholic Boy Blues: A Poet's Journal of Healing* (2015), *Songs in Sepia and Black and White* (2012), and *Bloodroot: Indiana Poems* (2008). In 2007, Acme Records released his poetry and jazz CD with pianist-composer Monika Herzig. He served as Indiana Poet Laureate from 2008-10.

DORIANNE LAUX grew up listening to Bob Dylan on a scratchy transistor radio and was both delighted and influenced by the poetry of his lyrics and the mystery of his persona. She divides her time between Raleigh, North Carolina, where she teaches in the MFA Program at NC State University, and Richmond, California. She is the author of six collections of poems, and the forthcoming *Only As The Day Is Long: New and Selected Poems*. With Kim Addonizio, she is the co-author of the celebrated textbook *The Poet's Companion: A Guide to the Pleasures of Writing Poetry (1997)*.

JIM LAVILLA-HAVELIN is the author of five books of poems, most recently, *West* (2017). An educator and retired arts administrator, he coordinates National Poetry Month in San Antonio and serves as Poetry Editor for the San Antonio *Express-News*. He lives in Lyle, Texas, outside San Antonio, with his wife, the artist, Lucia LaVilla-Havelin.

RICHARD LEVINE, a retired teacher and activist, is the author of *Contiguous States*, *The Cadence of Mercy,* and *A Tide of a Hundred Mountains*. He lives in Brooklyn, home of attitude and the VA hospital where Dylan visited an ailing Woody Guthrie.

M. L. LIEBLER is the author of fifteen books and chapbooks, including *Wide Awake in Someone Else's Dream* (2008), recipient of The Paterson Poetry Prize for Literary Excellence and The American Indie Book Award for 2009. *Working Words: Punching the Clock & Kicking Out the Jams* (2010) received a 2011 Library of Michigan Notable Book Award. In 2017, Liebler received two Library of Michigan Notable Book Awards for his new collection of poems, *I Want to Be Once* (2016), and for *Heaven Was Detroit: An Anthology of Detroit Music Essays from*

Jazz to Hiphop (2016). He has taught English, Creative Writing, American Studies, Labor Studies, and World Literature at Wayne State University in Detroit since 1980. He has recorded and worked with Al Kooper, Bob Dylan's organist, for twenty years.

LYN LIFSHIN has published over one hundred and thirty books, most recently: *Little Dancer: The Degas Poems* (2017); *Alive Like a Loaded Gun* (2016); *Malala* (2014); *Secretariat* (2014); *Femme Eterna* (2014); and *A Girl Goes into the Woods: Selected Poems* (2013). She remembers seeing Dylan at Gerde's Folk City in the West Village and that the audience there that night thought Dylan was weird and awful, but she liked him right away. Lifshin lives in Virginia.

LAURINDA LIND lives and works in New York's North Country, where it's hardly worth bothering to put coats away after spring. Her work has appeared in *Antithesis*, *Barbaric Yawp*, *Chiron Review*, *Cold Mountain Review*, *Communion*, *The Comstock Review*, *Ellipsis*, *Liminality*, *Mobius*, *Ship of Fools*, *Silver Birch Press*, *Triggerfish*, *Uproot*, and *Veil*.

LACHLAN MACKINNON was born in Aberdeen, Scotland, and educated at Charterhouse and Christ Church, Oxford. He is the author of *Doves* (2017); *Small Hours* (2010), shortlisted for the 2010 Forward Poetry Prize; *The Jupiter Collisions* (2003); *The Coast of Bohemia* (1991); and *Monterey Cypress* (1988). Upon retirement from Winchester College, where he taught English for many years, he moved to Ely, Cambridgeshire, and reviews regularly for the *Times Literary Supplement*.

C. P. MANGEL is the author of *Laundry* (2015), a chapbook. She was counsel for a pharmaceutical company for over twenty years, and then received her MFA in Creative Writing from the University of British Columbia. She lives in North Carolina with her husband, four adult children, and her rescue muses, a pit bull and a rat terrier.

GARY MARGOLIS is Emeritus Executive Director of College Mental Health Services as well as Associate Professor of English and American Literatures (part-time) at Middlebury College. He was a Robert Frost and Arthur Vining Davis Fellow and has taught at the Universities of Tennessee and Vermont and Bread Loaf, and Green Mountain Writers' Conferences. His recent books are *Runner Without a Number* (2016) and *Raking the Winter Leaves: New and Selected Poems* (2013). *Time Inside*, poems centered on his poetry workshop in a maximum security prison, is forthcoming. He shares Bob Dylan's birthdate, May 24.

DEBRA MARQUART is the author of six books, including *Small Buried Things: Poems* (2015), *The Horizontal World: Growing Up Wild in the Middle of Nowhere* (2007), and a co-edited anthology of experimental writing, *Nothing to Declare: A Guide to the Prose Sequence* (2016). She teaches nonfiction in the Stonecoast MFA program at the University of Southern Maine, and directs the MFA Program in Creative Writing and Environment at Iowa State University. Her work has been featured on three NPR programs—*Morning Edition, The Writer's Almanac*, and *On Point*—and the BBC.

MICHAEL MCCLURE, poet, playwright, songwriter and novelist, taught English for many years at what is now California College of the Arts. He was among the poets who read at the legendary

Six Gallery reading in San Francisco in 1955. Among his more than fifty books are *Persian Pony* (2017), *Mephistos and Other Poems* (2016), *Of Indigo and Saffron: New and Selected Poems* (2011), and *Scratching the Beat Surface* (1994). He has collaborated with the Doors' keyboardist, Ray Manzarek, recording the CDs *The Piano Poems: Live in San Francisco* (2012), *The Third Mind* (2006), *There's a Word* (2001), and *Love Lion* (1993). You can hear him read from Chaucer in Martin Scorsese's *The Last Waltz*, and he co-wrote the song "Mercedes Benz" with Janis Joplin and Bob Neuwirth. You can find McClure hanging out with Bob Dylan, Allen Ginsberg, and Robbie Robertson in a photograph by Larry Keenan taken in the alley behind City Lights Books in 1965. He lives in the San Francisco Bay Area.

LINDA BACK MCKAY is a poet, author, writing coach, and teaching artist. Her poetry books include *The Next Best Thing* (2011) and *Ride That Full Tilt Boogie* (2001). Her nonfiction books include *Out of The Shadows: Stories of Adoption and Reunion* (2012), which inspired the play, *Watermelon Hill* produced by the History Theatre in St. Paul; and *Shadow Mothers* (1998). Bob Dylan was one of her first creative influences, and yes, she does know all the words of his early songs.

BILL MEISSNER's tribute to Dylan is from his new manuscript of poems, *The Mapmaker's Dream*. Among Meissner's eight books are four books of poetry, including *American Compass* (2004) and *Twin Sons of Different Mirrors: Poems in Dialogue with Jack Driscoll* (1993). He lives in St. Cloud, Minnesota. He's a huge Dylan fan (and does a decent voice impersonation), and was the featured speaker on Literary Night at Dylan Days in Hibbing, Minnesota.

MICHAEL MINGO is an adjunct professor at The Johns Hopkins University in Baltimore, MD. His work has most recently appeared in *The Louisville Review* and *Glassworks*. He has been a fan of Bob Dylan's music since his sophomore year of high school, and he uses Dylan's lyrics in the classroom as examples of the ballad tradition.

PAUL MULDOON is an Irish poet and professor of poetry, as well as an editor, critic, and translator. Muldoon is the author of twelve collections of poetry, including: *Selected Poems: 1968-2014* (2016), *One Thousand Things Worth Knowing* (2015), *Maggot* (2010), *Horse Latitudes* (2006), and *Moy Sand and Gravel* (2002), winner of the 2003 Pulitzer Prize for Poetry. Rogue Oliphant, a loose affiliation of musicians and composers who work on songs and spoken word pieces written by Muldoon, released their first CD, *I Gave the Pope a Rhino*, in 2016. He served as poetry editor of the *New Yorker* from 2007-2017. *Sadie and the Sadists*, a collection of sixteen punk-rock-style song lyrics by Muldoon, was published in 2017.

KATIE DARBY MULLINS teaches creative writing at the University of Evansville. In addition to being nominated for a Pushcart Prize and editing a rock 'n' roll crossover edition of the metrical poetry journal *Measure*, she's been published or has work forthcoming in *Hawaii Pacific Review*, *Harpur Palate*, *Prime Number*, and *The Evansville Review*. She's the lead writer and founder of the music blog *Katie Darby Recommends*.

EILEEN MYLES, poet, novelist, performer, and art journalist, has published more than twenty books, including *Afterglow (a dog memoir) (2017)*; a 2017 re-issue of *Cool for You* (a novel) and *I Must Be*

Living Twice: New and Selected Poems (2016), and *Chelsea Girls*, a novel (2015). Myles's other books include *Snowflake/different streets* (2012), *Inferno: A Poet's Novel* (2010), *The Importance of Being Iceland: Travel Essays in Art* (2009). From 1984-1986, Myles served as artistic director of the St. Mark's Poetry Project in New York City. .

TIM NOLAN was born in Minneapolis, graduated from the University of Minnesota with a B.A. in English, and from Columbia University in New York City with an MFA in writing. He is the author of three collections of poems, most recently *The Field* (2016). He has loved Dylan since first hearing "Blowin' in the Wind" on the radio in 1963.

JENI OLIN received her BA and MFA from Naropa University. Her full-length collections of poems include *Hold Tight: The Truck Darling Poems* (2010) and *Blue Collar Holiday* (2005), with full color original drawings by Larry Rivers. She is also the author of *The Pill Book* (2008), a chapbook of pharmaceutical sonnets about antidepressants. She lives in Manhattan.

LISA PANEPINTO lives in Pittsburgh, PA. She is the author of *On This Borrowed Bike* (2014) and poetry editor for *Cabildo Quarterly*. As a teenager she often borrowed the CD *Bob Dylan Live 1966-Bootleg Series Vol. 4-The "Royal Albert Hall" Concert* from the Spokane Public Library and was transported by the imagistic, raw, and emotional album. Dylan continues to be one of her greatest poetic and musical influences.

LINDA PASTAN, former Poet Laureate of Maryland (1991-1995), is the author of more than fifteen books of poetry, among them, *A Dog Runs Through It* (2018), *Insomnia: Poems* (2015), *Traveling Light: Poems* (2011), *Carnival Evening. New and Selected Poems:1968 –1998* (1998), a finalist for the National Book Award. She lives in Chevy Chase, Maryland.

DAVID PICHASKE is Professor of English at Southwest State University in Minnesota. He has published over two dozen books, starting with the poetry anthology *Beowulf to Beatles: Approaches to Poetry* (1972) through to *A Generation in Motion: Popular Music and Culture in the 1960s* (1979), and, most relevant here, *Song of the North Country: A Midwest Framework to the Songs of Bob Dylan* (2010). *Here I Stand*, a memoir, was published in 2015. He lives on a gravel road outside of Granite Falls, Minnesota.

CATHERINE PIERCE is the author of three books of poems: *The Tornado Is the World* (2016), *The Girls of Peculiar* (2012), and *Famous Last Words* (2008). Her poems have appeared in *The American Poetry Review, The Best American Poetry*, *Ploughshares*, and elsewhere. She lives in Starkville, Mississippi, where she is an associate professor of English at Mississippi State University. Her early twenties were scored almost entirely to *Blood on the Tracks* and *Blonde on Blonde*.

LIZA PORTER's poetry chapbook *Red Stain* (2014) was a finalist for both the 2015 New Mexico-Arizona Book Award and the 2015 WILLA Award (Women Writing the West). Porter received the 2009 Mary Ann Campau Memorial Poetry Fellowship from the University of Arizona Poetry Center. She is founding director of the Other Voices Women's Reading Series at Antigone Books in Tucson, Arizona. Her essays and poetry have been published in numerous magazines, including *AGNI, Barrow Street, Cimarron Review, Passages North, and PRISM International*, and in the anthologies *What Wildness is this: Women Write About the Southwest,* and *Poets on Prozac: Mental Illness, Treatment and the Creative Process.*

CAROL KAPAUN RATCHENKSI, a North Dakota native, is a counselor, compassionate communication trainer, mom, writer, sister, friend, and poet. Her work has appeared in the *North Dakota Quarterly, NDSU Magazine*, and *North Country*. Her work has also been published in the anthologies *Resurrecting Grace: Remembering Catholic Childhoods* and *The Cancer Poetry Project*. She is the founder of The Center for Compassion and Creativity, a private-practice counseling center. Her collection of poems, *A Beautiful Hell*, was published in 2016.

JOHN REINHARD is the author of two poetry collections, *On the Road to Patsy Cline* (1996) and *Burning the Prairie* (1988). He teaches at South Central College in Faribault, Minnesota, and lives with his family in nearby Owatonna.

ELLEN SANDER, a pioneering New York rock journalist, author of *Trips: Rock Life in the Sixties* (1973), incubated her poetry in Bolinas, California, in the seventies. She served as Poet Laureate of Belfast, Maine, in 2013 and 2014. Her poetry has been published in *Chiron Review, Social Anarchism, Saturday Afternoon Journal* and others, and in the chapbooks *Stand of Herons* and *Craters*. She is on the board of the Belfast Poetry Festival and a member of Beyond Baroque.

JUDITH SANDERS holds a B.A. in literature from Yale, an M.A. in fiction writing from Boston University, and a Ph.D. in English from Tufts. She is the recipient of the 2012 Hart Crane Memorial Poetry Contest sponsored by Kent State University. Her creative and scholarly work has appeared in many journals, including *The American Scholar*, *Independent Teacher*, and *Film Quarterly*, and the *Pittsburgh Post-Gazette*. A former Fulbright Scholar to France, Sanders currently teaches at Winchester Thurston School in Pittsburgh.

PATTI SMITH, writer, performer, visual artist, is the author of twenty books, including *M Train* (2015) and the memoir *Just Kids* (2010), winner of a 2010 National Book Award. Her recordings include *Banga* (2012), *Twelve* (2007), *Easter* (1978), and *Horses* (1975), hailed by *Rolling Stone* as one of the top 100 albums of all time. In 2007, she was inducted into the Rock and Roll Hall of Fame. On 10 December 2016, Smith attended the Nobel Prize Award Ceremony in Stockholm on behalf of Bob Dylan, winner of the Nobel Prize in Literature. Smith sang Dylan's "A Hard Rain's A-Gonna Fall." In December of 1995, Smith and her band opened for Dylan on the ten-date "Paradise Lost Tour" and joined Dylan on stage to duet on "Dark Eyes."

GERARD SMYTH is an Irish poet, critic, and journalist living in Dublin. He has published ten collections of poetry, including *The Yellow River* (2017), *A Song of Elsewhere* (2015), and *The Fullness of Time: New and Selected Poems* (2010). He was the 2012 recipient of the O'Shaughnessy Poetry Award presented by the University of St. Thomas in Minnesota and is co-editor, with Pat Boran, of *If Ever You Go: A Map of Dublin in Poetry and Song* (2014). His essay

"Is Bob Dylan really a poet?" appeared in the *Irish Times* in 2011 and has since been reprinted in many European newspapers and magazines.

TIMOTHY STEELE's most recent book of poems is *Toward the Winter Solstice* (2006). His literary criticism includes a study of versification, *All the Fun's in How You Say a Thing* (1999). An emeritus professor at California State University, Los Angeles, he was born and raised in Burlington, Vermont. "The Concert" records his memories of Bob Dylan's performance in Burlington at the Roy L. Patrick Gymnasium on Saturday evening, 23 October 1965.

J. J. STEINFELD, Canadian fiction writer, poet, and playwright, lives on Prince Edward Island, where he is patiently waiting for Godot's arrival and a phone call from Kafka. While waiting, he has published eighteen books, including *Absurdity, Woe Is Me, Glory Be* (2017), *An Unauthorized Biography of Being* (2016), *Madhouses in Heaven, Castles in Hell* (2015), and *Identity Dreams and Memory Sounds* (2014).

HEATHER STEINMANN received her MFA in Creative Writing from Minnesota State University Moorhead and her Ph.D in Writing, Rhetoric, and Culture from North Dakota State University. Her writing has been published in *Up the Staircase Quarterly*, *Eclectica Magazine*, **82 Review*, and the TedX Fargo Poetry Broadside Series. She is Assistant Professor of English in the Department of Humanities at Western New Mexico University.

MARTY STERNSTEIN grew up in what was then called The West Bronx, then moved a couple of stops down to Greenwich Village. Dylan was rising and Marty was watching, nine years his senior. For decades he wrote only sporadically, expending and replenishing his energies teaching young people in several different schools, mostly in Manhattan. For the last ten years he's been writing. Chapbooks of verse and one-act plays include *Oblivious to Shapes* (2012) and *Can Timmy Come Out and Play?* (2012).

JOYCE SUTPHEN grew up on a farm in Stearns County, Minnesota. Her first collection of poems, *Straight Out of View*, won the Barnard New Women Poets Prize (1995). Recent collections of poems include *The Green House* (2017) and *Modern Love and Other Myths* (2015), a finalist for a Minnesota Book Award. She is the second Minnesota Poet Laureate, succeeding Robert Bly. She has been listening to Dylan for more than a half-century.

JUDY SWANN is a poet, essayist, translator, mom, blogger, and bicycle commuter, whose work has been published in many venues both in print and online. Her book, *We Are All Well: The Letters of Nora Hall* (2014), has given her great joy. She lives in Ithaca, NY.

RUSSELL THORBURN is the author of *Somewhere We'll Leave the World* (2017) and songwriter/musician for a sextet called Radio On, which lays down electric landscapes in sound and spoken word. His poem included in the anthology is an homage to Big Pink and Bob Dylan. He lives in Marquette, MI.

CHRYS TOBEY lives in Portland, OR, where she teaches college writing. Her poems have appeared in many literary journals, including the *minnesota review*, *New Ohio Review*, *Ploughshares*, *Rattle*, and *The Cincinnati Review*. Her first full-length book of poems, *A Woman is a Woman is a Woman is a Woman*, was published in 2017.

RODNEY TORRESON was the poet laureate of Grand Rapids, Michigan, from 2007-2010. Author of four books, his latest is *The Secrets of Fieldwork* (2010), a chapbook of poems. Other collections include *The Ripening of Pinstripes: Called Shots on The New York Yankees* (1998) and *A Breathable Light* (1992).

KATRINA VANDENBERG bought her first copy of Bob Dylan's *Blood on the Tracks* as a teenager. She is most recently the author of *The Alphabet Not Unlike the World* (2012). She is a professor in The Creative Writing Programs at Hamline University, where she also serves as Poetry Editor for *Water~Stone Review*. She lives with her family in St. Paul, MN.

ANNE WALDMAN is the author of more than sixty books of poetry, among them *Extinction Aria* (2017), *Voice's Daughter of a Heart Yet To Be Born* (2016), *Jaguar Harmonics* (2014), *In the Room of Never Grieve: New & Selected Poems 1985–2003* (2003), and the iconic *Fast Speaking Woman and Other Chants* (1975; revised edition, 1978). In 1976, she traveled through New England and Canada as a member of Dylan's *Rolling Thunder Revue* and was featured in Dylan's film, *Renaldo and Clara* (1978). In 2015, the Before Columbus Foundation honored Waldman with the American

Book Award's Lifetime Achievement Award. In 2011, Waldman was elected a Chancellor of the Academy of American Poets. With Chogyam Trungpa Rinpoche, Allen Ginsberg, and others, Waldman founded the The Jack Kerouac School of Disembodied Poetics at the Naropa Institute (now Naropa University), where she remains a Distinguished Professor of Poetics and the Director of Naropa's Summer Writing Program.

CONNIE WANEK is retired from the Duluth Public Library and now spends her time in New Mexico as well as Minnesota. Her most recent book of poems is *Rival Gardens: New and Selected Poems* (2016). She has friends who live in a house Bob Dylan built and where he lived for a time.

MICHAEL WATERS is the author of numerous collections of poems, most recently *Celestial Joyride* (2016), *Gospel Night* (2011), and *Darling Vulgarity* (2006), a finalist for the *Los Angeles Times* Book Prize. His work has appeared in numerous journals, including *American Poetry Review*, *Kenyon Review*, *Paris Review*, *Poetry*, *Rolling Stone*, and *Yale Review*.

DAVID WOJAHN was born in St. Paul, Minnesota. His most recent collections of poems include *For the Scribe* (2017), *World Tree* (2011), and *Interrogation Palace: New and Selected Poems 1982-2004* (2006), a finalist for the Pulitzer Prize for Poetry. Wojahn is the author of two collections of essays on contemporary poetry, *From the Valley of Making: Essays on the Craft of Poetry* (2015) and *Strange Good Fortune* (2001); co-editor of *A Profile of Twentieth Century American Poetry* (1991); and editor of two posthumous collections of poems of his wife Lynda Hull's poetry, *The Only World* (1995) and *Collected*

Poems (2006). He is presently Professor of English at Virginia Commonwealth University and is also a member of the program faculty of the MFA in Writing Program of Vermont College of the Fine Arts.

ANNE HARDING WOODWORTH is the author of five books, the most recent being the chapbook *The Last Gun* (2016), and *Unattached Male* (2014). Harding Woodworth sits on the Poetry Board of the Folger Shakespeare Library, Washington DC, where she lives when she is not at her cabin in the mountains of Western North Carolina.

BARON WORMSER is the author/co-author of fourteen books, including most recently the novel *Tom o' Vietnam* (2017) and a collection of poems, *Unidentified Sighing Objects* (2015). He has received fellowships from the National Endowment for the Arts, Bread Loaf, and the John Simon Guggenheim Memorial Foundation. He lives in Montpelier, Vermont, where he can be found listening to the complete *Basement Tapes*. He is working on a book-length fiction about a character who bears a resemblance to Bob Dylan.

CHARLES WRIGHT is the author of more than twenty collections of poetry, most recently *Caribou* (2014); *Bye-and-Bye: Selected Late Poems* (2011); *Outtakes* (2010); and *Sestets: Poems* (2009). *Black Zodiac* (1997) was awarded the 1998 Pulitzer Prize for Poetry, and *Country Music: Selected Early Poems* (1983) shared the 1983 National Book Award with Galway Kinnell's *Selected Poems*. His collections of prose include *Quarter Notes: Improvisations and Interviews* (1995), and *Halflife: Improvisations and Interviews, 1977-1987* (1988). Wright served as U.S. Poet Laureate in 2014-15.

LISA ZARAN is the author of six collections of poems, including *Dear Bob Dylan* (2015), *If It We* (2012), and *The Blondes Lay Content* (2006). Zaran is founder and editor of *Contemporary American Voices*, an online journal of poetry, now in its eleventh year. Zaran began listening to Bob Dylan as a young adult and credits his work as the most influential poems in her life. She lives in Arizona and works in the municipal court system.

PERMISSIONS

Title Index

About New Rivers Press

New Rivers Press emerged from a drafty Massachusetts barn in winter 1968. Intent on publishing work by new and emerging poets, founder C. W. "Bill" Truesdale labored for weeks over an old Chandler & Price letterpress to publish three hundred fifty copies of Margaret Randall's collection *So Many Rooms Has a House but One Roof* (1968). About four hundred titles later, New Rivers is now a nonprofit learning press, based since 2001 at Minnesota State University Moorhead. Charles Baxter, one of the first authors with New Rivers, calls the press "the hidden backbone of the American literary tradition."

As a learning press, New Rivers guides student editors, designers, writers, and filmmakers through the various processes involved in selecting, editing, designing, publishing, and distributing literary books. In working, learning, and interning with New Rivers Press, students gain integral real-world knowledge that they bring with them into the publishing workforce at positions with publishers across the country, or to begin their own small presses and literary magazines.

Please visit our website: newriverspress.com for more information.